HIDDEN
CHESHIRE

J. Brian Curzon

Other Cheshire titles available from Countryside Books include:

CHESHIRE PRIVIES
J. Brian Curzon

CHESHIRE: A PORTRAIT IN COLOUR
Bill Meadows

WATERSIDE WALKS IN CHESHIRE
James F. Edwards

PUB WALKS IN CHESHIRE
James F. Edwards

CHESHIRE RAILWAYS REMEMBERED
Leslie Oppitz

HIDDEN
CHESHIRE

J. Brian Curzon

COUNTRYSIDE BOOKS
NEWBURY, BERKSHIRE

COUNTRYSIDE BOOKS
3 Catherine Road
Newbury, Berkshire

To view our complete range of books,
please visit us at
www.countrysidebooks.co.uk

ISBN 1 85306 651 6

The front cover photograph of Knutsford
and the back cover photograph of 'The Bridestones',
above Congleton were both taken by Bill Meadows

Designed by Graham Whiteman

Produced through MRM Associates Ltd., Reading
Printed in England by J.W. Arrowsmith Ltd., Bristol

INTRODUCTION

Those old times, those old times,
Some say that they were bad,
But I think that those old times,
Were anything but sad,
Then banners waved o'er Beeston's wall,
Then clarion sounded loud,
As Cheshire sprang to honour's call,
Cheshire's midst, the proudest proud.

Egerton Leigh's *Cheshire Ballads and Legends*

Cheshire has an identity crisis. Until 1974 you knew where it was and what it looked like. It was like a teapot with the Wirral as a spout and a broken handle in the east. The Maud report had tried to get rid of it and to give parts to the three big cities - and then the men in grey suits changed their plans. Much of Wirral went to a new Merseyside and the broken handle to Greater Manchester. Wilmslow won a hard fight to remain 'Cheshah'. They gave us Warrington and Widnes which had always been proudly 'Lankysheer' and they kept their Lancashire postmarks. Places like Stalybridge and Hyde hung on to their Cheshire ones in Greater Manchester. A TV quiz asked what county Warrington was in and when the contestant answered 'Cheshire' it was declared wrong. Many Warrington folk wrote to protest and the shamefaced quizmaster pointed out the following week all their letters were postmarked 'Warrington Lancashire'. Now Warrington and Halton (Runcorn and Widnes) have gone their own way. They are no longer administered by the County Council but are still in the geographic county; like it or not!

So, how does someone writing a book decide on what and where is actually Cheshire. I decided to be like a cook preparing a good meal and I have dipped into former Cheshire, for spice and garnish, if there is a tasty tale to tell. It is neither definitive nor exclusive and what is to my taste might not be to others. Some well known places are included if there was a tale or something which needed explaining. So, what do I call 'hidden'? It obviously does not imply that someone has deliberately hidden anything so that no one can find it, but places and things which are out of the way or not widely known about outside the locality. In fact I prefer to think more in terms of 'the secrets of Cheshire'. Places I have included are not just obscured by being in the heart of the country, but sometimes in the depths of busy towns. Some are well known to the people living near to them but not by those from another town. Having said that, in researching this I have spoken to librarians, conservation officers and clergymen who have not had the slightest inkling of things which I have taken as common knowledge.

Anywhere, in fact, where traces from past ages linger or there is a story to tell has been worth investigating. Many stories and legends have more than one version and I make no claims that any given here are the only ones, much less the one true version, but more those which I think you will enjoy.

I first started to explore my home county in the 1950s and while I have made every possible attempt to check that things are as described, things that have been in the same place for hundreds of years can and do get moved or destroyed. Usually when I decide to write about them or take people to see them! I must thank Peter Hammil-Stewart for acting as my driver and managing to find all these obscure places so that I could be sure that what I claimed was 'in the middle of fields' still was and not now surrounded by an industrial estate! If I have given overmuch to the middle of the plain it is because that is and always has been my home and it is an area about which I know most and know the obscure tales the best.

Cheshire, of whatever shape you choose, remains a strange place to write about. I was once introduced to the Sheriff of Nottingham (yes, they still have one!) and told him I came from Cheshire. 'Oh! The County of Snobs!' he responded. Well yes, there are plenty of them in the county; it is said to be the richest and best heeled shire county. The claim that there are more Rolls Royces and millionaires in some parts than any similar area on earth may no longer be true, as today's wealthy prefer something less cumbersome and showy than a Rolls; although you often see new ones being tested near their factory in Crewe. More earned their money by their own endeavours in modern fields like technology, sport or pop music than inherited it with a title and lands.

On the other hand it has had its 'unemployment blackspots' with its fair share of social problems. Politically it is a mixture of bright red and deep blue. Somewhere it changes identity. Nantwich, Chester and Tarporley belong to the green Welsh borderlands, but Macclesfield, Warrington or Runcorn are truly

Northern and Mottram in Longdendale was the home of the most important of all Northern painters, L.S. Lowry. It is a subtle change. You can't claim to know Cheshire unless you have ridden through the hills near the Wildboarclough and watched the sunset over the sands of Dee. You must see pretty villages in the south and back streets in industrial towns; amongst the biggest in England - it is a county of contradictions. Many people dismiss it as flat and boring but it has the Cat and Fiddle, known as the second highest pub, Beeston as the most impressive castle site in England and places like Stockport and Macclesfield where every street seems to be on a hill. There are busy night-clubs and large stores or hidden hamlets; more motorways than any other shire or peaceful one-track country lanes and canals to explore - and it is all Cheshire.

Take this, then, as an appetiser, set out yourself to find the things listed, and you will find so very, very much more of what, in parts at least, still deserves to be called England's Greenest County. Not that it is always green. In May the 'thunderflowers' of the hawthorn hedges and the wild parsley in the verges fill the air with scent and turn the lanes white. In October the hills and lanes take on wonderful shades of autumn, but in winter the image is often grey or brown when westerly winds bring rain clouds or frost and fogs cover the fields when the hawthorns and trees are dark and bare. Despite much that is modern there is still much that is old, attractive and curious, both in the country lanes and in its busiest towns that tells of a proud heritage. Little hereabouts is as simple as it seems, stories and curios are found all over the place. Let me introduce you to hidden Cheshire; keep this book with you as a companion and once you start to look you will be amazed by the things you will discover.

J. Brian Curzon

HIDDEN
CHESHIRE

ACTON

Acton's old church had to be repaired after playing its part in the Civil War battle of Nantwich in 1643 but is still full of interest including fine monuments of Sir William Mainwaring, who left a fragment of the true cross to the Church when he died in 1399, and Richard Wilbraham with his wife. They saw their lovely Dorfold Hall turned into the centre of the battle. There is a tall churchyard sundial: many churches have sundials, they were not just to tell the time or set the church tower clock, but also to remind folk of passing hours until they joined those in the churchyard. An inscription on this says just that, reminding you that 'tempus fugit' (time flies).

There is the grave here of someone who knew a thing or two about cricket, for a stone depicting a cricket bat, wickets and bails records Albert Hornby who died in 1925. He was captain of the English cricket team of 1882 who played so badly against Australia that the bails were ceremoniously burned - and have been played for ever since as 'The Ashes'.

The interior of the church contains an unusual feature in a seat running around the wall, no more than a ledge, and said to date from the days when there were no proper seats in churches. It was provided for the elderly or sick and is one of only twelve to survive in the country. Such provision was the origin of the saying, 'the weakest go to the wall'. There are old stones from an earlier church, including Saxon carvings of saints, amongst them two bishops with crosiers. The ancient Norman font was one of many in Cheshire found in a farmyard and used for pigswill, this one on the farm adjoining Dorfold Hall. During the Commonwealth the Puritans ordered that all fonts should be destroyed and replaced by small bowls for baptisms. They were duly taken from the churches but many found new uses as feeders for holding pigswill; which seemed more derogatory than simply breaking them up. In the Victorian period everything Gothic was back in fashion and many fonts were rescued from gardens or pigsties to be returned with honour to the church.

Dorfold Hall is a private residence built in 1616, but you can visit on certain days in the summer and see the stunning plasterwork of the main ceiling and a room traditionally prepared for a visit by James I, who never came. The font was not the only treasure in the farmyard for in the house is a splendid charger plate made by Thomas Toft, the greatest of all the slip-ware potters, decorated with the royal arms of King Charles II. It was found being used to feed chickens! The Nantwich Show, with its famous cheese section - said to be the biggest in the world - is held in the park each year. Nearby , in a field in a hamlet called Bluestone, is a large boulder polished smooth by the ice that left it there over 10,000 years ago. According to tradition, the Devil threw it at the church in a rage when it was being built.

ACTON BRIDGE

The prophet Nixon was born in Over and according to legend died because he was called to the royal court, where he had foreseen he would die of starvation. This actually happened, because he made such a nuisance of himself pinching food that he was locked up and forgotten about. He once said Vale Royal Abbey and Norton Priory would meet in the middle of the River Weaver. It came true when a new bridge was built using the stone from both at Acton Bridge. The canalised part of the river is crossed by an iron swing bridge resting on an island in the centre but the 'old river' next to it is still crossed by the stone bridge that Nixon prophesied.

By the station the Hazel Pear pub keeps the name of a particular local variety which is now almost impossible to buy because of EEC regulations. The Campaign for Real Ale tried to keep the Holly Bush Inn (Bartington) as a simple farmhouse which also served beer, but change was inevitable. Now its old farm buildings are converted to a motel, though the outside looks very much as it has always been, an attractive thatched black and white cottage dating from the 17th century.

ADLINGTON

The old house of one branch of the Legh family shows two faces to the world, one a lovely half-timbered manor and the other a formal 18th century classical facade. It is open to the public on certain days each year when its great hall can be seen rich with medieval heraldry and baroque wall paintings of classical scenes. One item which might be missed is a framed piece of 18th century music manuscript. It is a hunting song which Handel composed while he was a guest here. After visiting the local smithy he came back inspired and on this fine old organ he composed a piece of music and called it *The Harmonious Blacksmith*.

The gardens of Adlington contain a few interesting items including a classical statue which probably represented the spirit of the River Tiber lying in its river bed with water flowing from an upturned urn. It now presides over a garden pool. There is also a little cottage in which the resident hermit lived in the 19th century, when they were employed by the great houses to make the countryside interesting along with the deer and cattle in the park. These hermits should not to be confused with the religious men of the Middle Ages, but were paid to look strange and decorative; a perfect job for someone who found other people too annoying to want to talk to them. Today the same sort of people live 'on the streets' in our great cities; at least the 19th century landowners made sure that they were well fed as well as decorative.

ALDERLEY EDGE

Alderley Edge is known as a place for the affluent to retire, with one of the oldest and wealthiest populations in the country. Yet there was no such place as Alderley Edge until the railway came and needed a name for its station. In the 1840s the railway company decided to make this area what it became. Anyone who had a house built of the right value, got a free pass in the form of a fob to hang on his watch chain. Of course the company got their returns with regular custom by wives, children, servants, tradesmen and visitors who also made their journeys on the railway network and would usually pay First Class.

The Edge itself, now protected by the National Trust, has produced evidence of one of the oldest settlements in Cheshire in the form of flint tools around 7,000 years old. Men also mined copper here, probably before the Romans, and many stone hammers have been found which were used to crush ore. No one can tell how old they are; the only other things that look anything like them are Red Indian tomahawks! The Edge has many well known tales including a legend of King Arthur's knights sleeping here; a story kept alive by the Wizard of the Edge Restaurant. A farmer from Mobberley was taking a fine white horse to sell at Macclesfield Market when he was stopped by the wizard, who took him through great iron doors into a cave where the knights were all asleep round the famous table. There were plenty of caves which were former mines and can be explored by arrangement, with the help of experienced guides - but only try it if you are sure you are fit enough. It has been suggested that the story of the wizard was brought to Alderley from Cornwall by Cornish miners who came to work here, for the mines had veins of copper and lead which were worth mining then before better deposits overseas were discovered.

There is also the wishing well in which the custom was to put bent pins if girls wanted husbands or children. Its inscription, like the stone circle close to it, is bogus. In the 19th century the railway made this area a Mecca for people from Manchester, who the locals termed 'Cottontots', to come to for an afternoon in the country and these curios were provided for the most gullible visitors by a local stonemason.

 # ALDERSLEY

Practically every community has its memorial to the dead of the First World War, but few can be more idyllic than the one here. This is no cold silent cenotaph, nor is it decorated with symbolic or dramatic figures. At first it looks something like a rather superior bus shelter with low stone walls supporting timber posts and a tiled roof on top, but inside is a water pump and a trough in which to stand the bucket. To the side are seats for people to rest before taking the water home, or just to talk and enjoy the quiet surroundings. There are few places which have escaped the post war changes so well as this lovely spot with a few old cottages overlooking the mill-pool from which the swans and ducks come to be fed.

There were only two men, both from the Aldersley family, to commemorate. Mark, who fell in France aged 17, and Hugh, who died in Palestine aged 24 and is buried on the Mount of Olives outside the city whose name translates as peace but has seen so many wars. There is a wood carving of the crest of Aldersley

Aldersley's unusual war memorial

inside. They could not have been marked in a more useful or pleasant way, where villagers collected their daily water from the pump, and I have found no better place in Cheshire to sit.

ALLOSTOCK

A little building on a corner has links with the growth of the British Empire and memories of men who gained their fame in foreign lands. During the 18th century the minister of the little Unitarian chapel here also had a school for boys. One of them was Robert Clive, who had been running a protection gang with his school friends terrifying shopkeepers in Shrewsbury with threats to break windows if they did not pay. He was sent here 'out of harm's way' to finish his education under the instruction of the Minister. Later he became one of the leading figures in the East India Company and partly responsible for India becoming part of the Empire. He revenged the scandal of 'the Black Hole of Calcutta', winning victory at Plassey in Bengal in 1757. Another ex-pupil was said to be General Wolfe who died taking the Heights of Abraham in 1759 in the decisive battle which made Canada British and not French. The flag in which his body was wrapped still hangs in Chester Cathedral. Today, the chapel is no longer used and has become a house; the Empire is no more and few who drive past would think that it owed so much to two boys who came to school here.

ALSAGER

——— You say the first part as *all*, the next as *say* and the last as in *Ger*man. The Georgian church was built by the Misses Alsager and is an attractive building with many classical urns. It was designed by Thomas Stringer, some say it was John. Was he the painter from Knutsford who was employed by Wedgwood to produce pictures of local beauty spots to be put on the great 'frog' dinner service he sent to the Empress of Russia? Despite early promise Stringer moved to Northwich and turned to drink - was the move the cause of the other? Yet the most attractive things to see here are bathroom fittings! The Caradon factory has its own little museum in the reception area. It is not open to the general public, but those interested in the history of design, sanitation or social history can make an appointment to view. It is a wonderful collection and is an art gallery in its own right. Many of the specimens are of moulded or printed clay and in a wide variety of designs in this unusual treasure house.

Today Alsagar is perhaps best known for its university campus, which was originally one of the colleges set up in former barracks for the emergency teaching of men who had left the forces after the Second World War. They were needed to teach the 'post war bulge' of children born to couples reunited after wartime separation. As befitted the spirit of the time they too were separated from the women students, who had their own college near Crewe.

ALTRINCHAM

It is a memory of the first few months of the First World War that is worth seeking out here. For King George V dubbed Chapel Street 'the bravest street in England' when 161 men out of only 60 houses in the entire street enrolled to fight. Thirty did not return and a telegram was sent at the King's command to thank the people of Altrincham. It is still kept at the Town Hall. A public subscription was raised and a cast iron frame containing a list of all 161 names was unveiled. It was part of the railings around All Saints church which was at the junction with Regent Road. The bravest street was demolished as below standard, and is now a car park, but the scroll of honour in its cast iron and glass case has been moved and restored close by.

An unexpected obstacle on the town's golf course is a complete moated site. Although it has been partly excavated by the local archaeology society who found prehistoric flints, which are regularly found when excavators look for later remains in Cheshire, they did not find much about what had stood on the moat. Moats were dug as much to drain clayish soils for house building as for defence and the clay dug from them was often used to make the wattle and daub or bricks for the house. They were useful as well as decorative, as household waste was poured into them and they were also used to keep fish for the table - real recycling and real organic food! Altrincham was once a great organic food production area as it was Manchester's version of 'the garden of England' in Kent. Altrincham carrots and onions were particularly well known 150 years ago when this was an important market gardening area depending on 'Manchester manure' which was carried from the overflowing privies of the city.

Altrincham was never a big place until the railways came, but is now a densely populated town. It was the subject of jokes in the 17th century. A Cheshire proverb says someone is 'like the Mayor of Altrincham who lies in bed when his breeches are mending' - implying he had only one pair. Another tells of:

> The mayor of Altrincham and the Mayor of Over,
> One's a thatcher, th'others a dauber (plasterer).

The tale is told of how the Mayor of Over went to meet the Mayor of Altrincham and feeling a bit grubby after his travels decided to call for a shave. He proudly told the barber that he could tell his customers that he had been allowed to shave the Mayor of Over. 'And you may tell the people of Over that you were shaved by the Mayor of Altrincham', came the proud reply.

 ## ANDERTON

Everyone who knows canals knows of Anderton and wants to make a pilgrimage to see the famous Boat Lift which was designed in 1873 to link the river in the valley with the Trent and Mersey Canal on a hilltop above. Restoration has just started using money from the National Lottery and soon you will be able to take a ride again. It is possible that James Brindley designed the canal to come so close as he was considering an inclined plane, along which boats would run on railway lines between the two. He died in 1772 before the link to Runcorn was completed and it appears that the Duke of Bridgewater scuppered any ideas that would avoid boats paying to use his locks in Runcorn.

From the start of the 19th century a trade developed transferring salt from the works on the Trent and Mersey into barges in the Weaver below, which could then be sailed direct to Liverpool. This avoided the hold ups in the tunnels and at Runcorn Locks that neither Brindley nor the Duke could have anticipated. They could never have guessed at the volume of trade that would be carried. The nearby Stanley Arms is known to all canal users simply as 'The Tip'. It is in fact very nice and tidy but got its name because it was there that the boat people rested when they had finished shovelling the salt from the narrow-boats into the long troughs which tipped it into the waiting barges on the river for the final leg of the journey into Liverpool, bypassing the tunnels and locks.

ANTROBUS

Beware if you come to this area in late October, for you might meet some strange people if you call in for a drink at one of the local pubs. For Antrobus is the home of the Soul Cake Play. Once almost every village in Cheshire had soulers. I think I must have been one of the last in Winsford, when we went round rather like carol singers begging for money for fireworks and singing the old song; 'If you haven't got a penny a ha'penny'll do, If you haven't got a ha'penny God bless you'. Antrobus saved an older tradition, which has two main sections. One is a play performed like a pantomime in which King George (probably originally Saint George) slays the Black Prince, who has a face painted black. His mother is like a pantomime dame and the Prince is cured by a 'Quack Doctor'. This is similar to mummers' plays which are usually performed in the spring, with its ideas of death and resurrection. The second part is a sort of auction of a horse, often called the Marbury Dunn, who in the performance only has three legs. Two are of the man inside, while the front leg supports a horse's skull which is specially wired so that it will snap its jaw, which can be quite frightening. Now Antrobus is a prosperous suburb of Warrington and the play is as likely to be performed by businessmen as farm labourers but the tradition lives on.

APPLETON

The thorn has been renewed several times, but the original was said to be a cutting from the famous one at Glastonbury where Joseph of Arimathea's staff miraculously took root to show him he had reached the place where the Holy Grail should rest. It was noted for flowering on Christmas Day, and on 29th June the villagers used to decorate it with ribbons and dance around it. The custom has been renewed around a replacement by the church and it has given its name to the local pub. No longer a village, but a suburb of Warrington there is also a very large Appleton Thorn School and even the Thorn Detention Centre for young offenders - they won't be seen dancing round the tree!

ARLEY GREEN

The little hamlet of Arley Green was created, as was Great Budworth, in the middle of the 19th century by Rowland Egerton Warburton, the rhyming squire of Arley, as a picture book of what he believed an old village should look like. He set up the well known rhyming signposts which can still be seen and converted an ancient timber-framed building to become one of the prettiest schools in the country. The children now go to Budworth, where the facilities are much better, but it still remains a charming and out of the way spot. One of his posts makes a useful link with the next entry:

> Trespassers this notice heed,
> Onward you may not proceed
> Unless to Arley Hall you speed.

ARLEY HALL

—— Arley Hall is well known and often used by television companies; it even has its own regular cookery and housekeeping series broadcast from the old barn. There is an irony in this as an 18th century cookery and housekeeping book was produced by Mrs Raffald who was housekeeper here.

In one of the rooms there is an engraving of Louis Napoleon of France. He was staying in exile here with a relative who rented the house while the owner was away on a tour of Europe. That was 1848, 'The Year of Revolutions' in Europe. He received the news of uprisings and left for France, where the unpopular Louis-Philippe was forced to abdicate. After a short time as President, Louis Napoleon became the Emperor. Bonaparte had had one son who became Napoleon II but did not survive. There are disputes about who exactly Louis Napoleon's father was and what his relationship was to the famous Napoleon. However, his time became known as the Second Empire and was a period of great rebuilding and artistic endeavour in Paris. Delacroix's famous painting of a woman holding the tricolour aloft in the ruins of Paris was inspired by the early stages of this Revolution - perhaps they should have a copy on show?

ASTBURY

—— The old church is one of the best known in Cheshire and is probably on a much more ancient place of worship, for a Bronze Age burial was found there. The village green is a well known delight when daffodils cover it. But the seeker of the strange looks in the churchyard at a set of old and worn monuments carved from sandstone and close to an old yew tree with a hole wide enough to walk through. On one is a tarnished brass plate with a story to tell. In the 17th century Sir Peter Leicester caused a storm when he declared that he could find no proof that Hugh Keveliok (there are many spellings), Earl of Chester, had been married. His daughter, Amica, was therefore probably a bastard. It caused outcry as most of the Cheshire gentry were in some way related. There was claim and counter claim, and someone put the brass plate here to say that those who were represented on the stone were Amica and her husband Sir Ralph Brereton, but the style of armour is much too late.

There is something else for seekers of the obscure. On the south side of the church look at the mortar, and you will see that the medieval masons used broken stained glass from the old church to make a damp proof course when building the new. Bits of medieval glass are peeping through where it has been weathered. They also used old gravestones, which can be spotted in various parts of the church walls.

ASTON BY SUTTON

On the edge of Runcorn you turn off from one of the busy roundabouts and find yourself back in another world. Pheasants ran across the road as I approached the church past the stump of a wayside cross. The ancient hall at Aston was pulled down in 1938 as it was just too big and costly for modern living. Even without it, the atmosphere is that of a country estate village. The old church survives. It replaced a much older private chapel and is a pleasant building of 17th and 18th century date and may have been designed by Vanbrugh. Actually some is less than 50 years old. We all know of the blitz in Liverpool, but even quiet country places in Cheshire suffered. A German bomb exploded next to Aston church and damaged much of it; you can still see bomb-damaged gravestones. When they returned from raids on Liverpool it was normal for the bombers to jettison any remaining bombs in the hope that they might hit something.

AUDLEM

By the imposing church is the 18th century Butter Market, just a roof on columns, and the 'bear stone' with a ring where they were tied for baiting. The glacial boulder was moved from the middle of the road junction when a memorial lamp was set up there.

Inside is the oddest thing to find in a Cheshire church - a Roman container for cremated ashes, shaped like an altar stone. It is carved with small portraits of Titia Charis who was 27 when she died, and her husband Titus Marius Alexander who commissioned it for their ashes. A former vicar brought it back from Rome, where it had been discovered near the Appian Way. Her hair-style indicates that it was made around AD 100. It now rests on a plinth in the Lady Chapel originally designed for a statue. Next to it is a huge board recording that James Holbrook, a Brewer of London in 1736, left the interest from an investment to pay for a regular service, sermon and bellringing in his memory. The remainder to be given in 'good wheaten bread' to the poor of Buerton where he was born - why not a drop of ale to go with it? Another oddity is the crown which once capped the village maypole and is placed above the north door.

The Shroppie Fly pub by the canal was converted from an old warehouse, with a bar created from half of an old narrow-boat and is worth a visit.

BADDILEY

Baddiley is indeed hidden at the end of a long country lane which just leads to the church and the old hall, now a farm. The church is a little timber structure, worth searching out for those interested in church history. In its medieval timber-framed walls are furnishings unchanged from the 18th century with box pews, each with their own door, and a three-decker pulpit. The parish clerk had the lower stage, the vicar took the Bible reading from the middle one before rising to the top for his sermon which could last an hour or two. The box pews not only kept out draughts but provided a little privacy. Above are the Mainwaring arms with those of Charles II, the Lord's Prayer, Creed and the Ten Commandments for those who might not have access to a book to read them. Perhaps one day special photography might confirm that there is a medieval painting of the Last Judgement with the Devil and the mouth of Hell, all painted over in post Reformation days. It must await scientific advances to enable us to see what has been obscured and not to damage the 17th century work.

 ## BARNTON

—— Known as 'Jam Town', Barnton once claimed to be the biggest village in England, a claim hotly disputed with Weaverham over the river, as both are the homes of those who work in Winnington and had more inhabitants than some towns. The disputes ceased with local government reorganisation in 1974 when the distinction between an Urban District and a Civil Parish ended. The village started to grow when the tunnel was built to take the Trent and Mersey away from Anderton to join the Duke of Bridgewater's canal at Preston Brook and trades associated with the canal developed. The first village shopkeeper was transported to Australia for stealing from the barges which were 'legged' through the tunnel by men lying on top of them, while the horses were taken over the top.

When Brunner Mond purchased land and helped some of the workers to pay for new houses to be built in the village by taking the weekly contribution from their wages, few working folk understood mortgages. Stories circulated that they had hardly any money to take home. Those who were jealous started the rumour that they were so much in debt that they only had jam butties for Sunday dinner. Local people still talk of 'goin' up th'ill ter Jam Town'.

 ## BARTHOMLEY

—— Barthomley is well known for the White Lion by the village church and a pretty collection of timber-framed houses which attract visitors on a summer evening to drive down twisting lanes and sit and enjoy the peace. It was not always peaceful; for one of the charges against Charles I was the Barthomley Massacre. When local men hid in the church tower during the Civil War, the Royalists made a bonfire of the rush mats from the church floor at the bottom and as the choking men emerged they were killed.

The church is believed to stand on a prehistoric burial mound and is the only ancient church dedicated to St Bertoline, who lived as a hermit on an island in the River Sow in Staffordshire. There are several good medieval effigies but it has one of the loveliest monuments in the shire. Lady Houghton married the son of a poet who later became Lord Crewe and died before her husband inherited that title. Her monument is a wonderful piece in the style known as 'New Sculpture'. She is shown, by the sculptor Sir Edgar Bohem, in white marble wearing a simple dress (for the 19th century at least) only decorated with a bit of lace, as if she is asleep.

BEBINGTON

Bebington has an old church with Norman work and Saxon stones. Robert Nixon, the prophet who had gloom and doom to say about most of Cheshire, claimed that if the ivy covered its spire it would herald the end of the world. Victorians watched the ivy grow ever higher with a Victorian air of impending doom until a lightning flash burnt it away. When it seemed to be advancing again a less stoic generation simply cut the whole lot down.

However, it is the Victorian Christ Church in Higher Bebington that students of the strange and unusual come to see. Above the door where we might expect to see a figure of a saint there is what locals call the Devil's footprints. In fact they are fossil prints of the *Chierotherium* (hand beast) and come from nearby Storeton Quarries which in their day produced more such footprints than anywhere else on earth. No one has yet found any bones of the reptile as bones do not survive as fossils in desert sands. Their footprints were preserved in thin layers of mud over which the sand blew, so we actually see a cast. They are early relatives of the dinosaurs and date from the Triassic Period around 250 million years ago. Scientists think they may have resembled the Kimodo dragons of Indonesia in appearance and habit, eating other animals and even their own kind. Many specimens are in the Liverpool Museum collection.

Although the footprints look like a hand, look closely and you will see the 'thumb' is on the outside. When the church was built in the 1850s even the best educated people had only just come to believe in dinosaurs and to try to get their tongues around the strange names. Darwin was yet to publish the theory of evolution and all Bibles still put the creation of the world as 4004 BC. No wonder people believed they were something to do with the Devil - at least he was in the Bible and ordinary people knew about him; while they could hardly comprehend the real story.

The town owes much to a Victorian jeweller, Joseph Mayer, whose shop in Liverpool became one of the city's treasure houses. He collected fine arts and craftsmanship from all periods, but especially Ancient Egypt, and two rooms at the back were set out as museum displays. When he died much of the collection passed to the Liverpool Museum, and amongst the items which still bear his name in their descriptions are the Mayer Mirror of decorated bronze, the Mayer Papyrus (a version of 'The Book of the Dead' from Ancient Egypt) and the Mayer Brooch, an exquisite example of the Anglo Saxon jeweller's art. He gave his home village a little library in a park, which was decorated with carvings representing learning, but this has now been replaced by a much larger building more appropriate for the busy town of today.

Also removed from the park wall, after it collapsed, are a group of stones with strange inscriptions. They are now in the Civic Centre where people can study them. Known as the 'Puzzle Stones', they have the sort of jokes that amused Victorians. One seemingly meaningless jumble of letters reads:

AR
UBB
I
NGS
TONEF
ORAS
SE
S

Made to look like a strange language, it was intended to make you look twice at what you see ('a rubbing stone for asses'). The stones were originally part of the old 'Two Crowns' pub and one of them makes use of the name with that of the landlord, Mark

Noble, to make a joke sum of adding the value of the old coins -
a mark (13s 4d), a noble (6s 8d) and two crowns (5 shillings each)

 ## Beeston

Beatrice Tunstall wrote of Beeston as 'the old grey monarch with a castle for a crown'. It is one of the most visited vantage points in Cheshire, now well maintained by English Heritage with a museum. The caves near the entrance are worth a mention for the fact that they were actually quarries for coarse sand, used to spread on the floor as scouring powder when brushing up. Of the castle little need be said as the museum and guide books tell you all; except the most fascinating. The square tower by the outer gate was the Wardrobe Tower where clothes were stored, washed and repaired. In its walls is a recess with a square drain - a primitive lavatory - but, most alarming, the drain actually has a window cut through it so that everything dropped from the arch at the top into a hole in the sill!

Something possibly remains hidden. Richard II stopped here on his way to Ireland, and is said to have left his treasure for safekeeping. He was arrested on his return and so could not retrieve it. Exploring the well, cavers found a chamber leading off to one side, presumed to be a sort of strong room. If the treasure was ever hidden there it had long since been removed. One of the adventurers who was lowered into the depths was Andrew Irvine, athletic son of the Cheshire antiquarian W.F. Irvine, who later lost his life attempting to climb Everest. Notice also that the walls are of stripes in two colours of stone. This Byzantine style of building was introduced from the East and reached its medieval best in the walls of Caernarvon. Later it was to gain favour even though John Ruskin (who championed its use) called it 'streaky bacon architecture'. It was also one of the first castles in England to be built without corners so that they could not be undermined.

I once organised a coach tour to include the 'Castles in the Clouds' at Beeston and Peckforton, and when we got there they actually were in the clouds. We climbed up the hill to see the wide views and could hardly see the person standing next to us! It gave a different perspective on what life must have been like for those who guarded the castle in days gone by and explained why Peckforton was used mainly for summer parties rather than as the family home.

Beeston is still famous for its market, although it no longer relies on the railway station, and deals in antiques as well as cattle. The Shropshire Union Canal passes through an unusual feature here, an iron lock designed by Thomas Telford. His canal was intended to join Nantwich and Chester, but the townsfolk of Nantwich did not want it to go into the town. Instead it ended at Acton, where it could be used to convey cheese but not salt adding to its decline as a salt town. In this area Telford encountered soft wet quicksand which would not support a structure made of stone or brick. To prevent collapsing he constructed Beeston Iron Lock out of cast iron sheets, probably inspired by the large evaporating pans he had seen in the salt works. The Chester canal alone was a complete failure because Nantwich could not be reached and Chester's days as a port were over. It eventually became important when additional branches were constructed to go to Middlewich and Shropshire and one terminating on the Mersey at Ellesmere Port. The name 'Shropshire Union' indicates a group of canals rather than one which unites two places. After trade on this canal ceased it found a new use as it was used to bring pure Welsh water to the taps of Crewe and Middlewich.

BELMONT CASTLE

A fantasy house by the turning from the A556 to Millington. Built of bright red brick, it is essentially an upper middle class Victorian house in fancy dress. Every detail has been given battlements to make it look like a fort. The outbuildings which contained a water-tank above look just like a castle with little turrets. Now abandoned, they look like the setting for a fairy tale with brambles growing from broken windows. The chimneys have been given battlements and the garden wall is most interesting of all. At each corner are little hearths with battlements in which fires were burnt, the flues passing through the garden walls so that fruit could be encouraged to grow. I was told that the Emperor of Ethiopia stayed there during the war, but nowhere could I find any details of its past.

BEWSEY

Perhaps it is my sense of humour but although I know full well that the origin of this place-name is 'beau isle' meaning 'beautiful island', it always makes me think of 'boozey' and to make matters worse the family that lived here were the Botelers; Lords of the Manor of Warrington. This might not seem quite so amusing if it was not so close to Warrington, known not so long ago for its three big breweries who used the artesian wells under the town. Of significance to anyone who has researched the 19th century is that Warrington was the first town to support a library out of the rates and one of the first to have a museum. Often brewers were totally against such places; thinking that the poor would sit in there where it was warm and light but where they did not need to spend a penny rather than sit in a warm pub buying their ale. Many pubs in those days included their own museums of stuffed birds and animals or other curios - an element of design which continues today - and provided books and newspapers. Warrington's own museum and library started in a pub! However, laughter aside, Bewsey Hall is one of the best preserved moated sites in this area with its old hall still standing. A proposal at one time to convert the old hall into Warrington's Peace Centre, following the IRA bombings in the town, did not materialise. There were too many restrictions on making use of the listed building and so a brand new centre where young people from all over the world can come together to discuss peaceful ends was built. The island in the moat at Bewsey was left to its own sort of peace.

BICKERTON HILLS

An outcrop of rock which is now National Trust property is the site of an ancient Iron Age camp, known as Maiden Castle, but not as grand as the Dorset version. At one time its stone ramparts, with traces of burnt wood inside, were believed to show it dated from just before the Romans came, but now archaeology has shown it was around 400 years older and possibly abandoned by then. We still do not know much, as the best archaeology is that which does not touch a thing. It is in a light woodland where the Trust takes great care that the special flora and fauna survive without invasions of inappropriate vegetation. A pleasant walk with information posts has been provided on paths specially covered to prevent eroding the soft sandstone.

The steep edges of the hills, all in a line with a little valley between, jutting sharply out of the plain, always remind me of the line from the hymn 'before the hills in order stood'. For in some places these hills look as if they have been carefully set out and neatly finished with a gigantic trowel. There are several caves in them which were given walls, windows and other comforts when they were used as homes in the 19th century. On one hillside at Gallantry Bank, a strange 'chimney' stands all on its own. It was actually a ventilator for a copper mine, and the nearby Copper Mine pub has photos and relics to tell of this almost forgotten local industry. There are far richer deposits of copper which are mined less expensively abroad and it would cost more to get the copper from Cheshire than it would be worth. It is romantically claimed that Gallantry derives its name from 'gallows tree' but many such gallows names can actually be traced to an old word 'gallas' which signified nothing more than ploughland.

BIDSTON

The hill was declared a place to be kept free of development when Birkenhead first started to grow, but less because of its amenity value than its use to Liverpool. Even before that port really took over from the ports on the Dee an old windmill had been used as a guide for shipping entering the Mersey, and still caps the hill. Then in 1771 a lighthouse was added for the same purpose. Until 1851 the hill was a mass of flagpoles, as signals were sent by semaphore all the way from Holyhead to Bidston. From there signals were sent by raising various flags into the port at Liverpool so that ship owners could be ready for when their ship arrived. In the days before radio links when vessels relied on good winds it was impossible to know when a ship would arrive. This advance warning allowed the owner to hire men at the dock gates ready to unload and reload the vessel, until it was replaced by a telegraph system in 1858.

In 1864 expansion of the Liverpool docks meant that the port's observatory was moved onto Bidston Hill with its main aims to give accurate time for Liverpool by observing the stars and to prepare weather forecasts. This was especially important as ships sometimes sailed out of the river into violent storms at sea. Until 1969 a noon cannon, operated from Bidston by telegraph, was fired at Birkenhead docks to let people in Liverpool set their clocks to aid navigation by the sun. Developments in calculating machines allowed construction of a clockwork apparatus which predicted tides at any part of the world. During the Second World War it was housed in a bomb proof underground room as it was from this Cheshire hilltop that the information on tides originated which allowed the famous Mulberry Harbours to be floated into place on D-Day.

Tam o'Shanter's Cottage, by the impressive Flaybrick Hill Cemetery, is thatched and whitewashed but has a relief representation of the flight of Tam, pursued by the witch 'Cutty Sark' (after whom the ship was named). According to Burns' poem, he only escaped by crossing a running stream. It has been restored as an outdoor education centre and every year a single pine cone must be paid in rent to the Mayor of Wirral for the right to use it.

Scratched into the sandstone, amidst numerous initials, are a figure of the sun and moon goddesses and a large horse. No one can be sure who engraved these figures or when they were made, but they simply add to the mystery of this old hill which is now surrounded by Merseyside's suburbia.

BIRCHWOOD

You will not find it on old maps for it was an invention of the Warrington New Town Corporation who were faced with one of the largest derelict sites in Europe. To make matters worse, a grim detention centre with a reputation for suicides was known throughout the land as 'Grisly Risley'. During the Second World War a factory at Risley was used to manufacture bombs and ammunition, but when peace was declared the factory, which had employed 30,000, was closed. Part of the area is an open space with pleasant walks, and Risley Moss is preserved as an important nature reserve, one of the finest surviving sites of its kind. The mounds above former bunkers where explosives were stored deep underground are used for children to play on. What used to be the factory reservoir is now a 'walled garden'. The name was changed to Birchwood as many young birches had sprung up in the dereliction and it is now known for its large stores, developed where there is plenty of parking space outside the town centre.

BIRKENHEAD

One of England's biggest towns, Birkenhead was originally intended to be an exclusive residential area for Liverpool merchants and stately Hamilton Square (based on those in Edinburgh) still reminds us of that era. Birkenhead had some remarkable firsts. It had the first public park, the first English flats (copied from Glasgow tenements for Glasgow folk who came to work in the shipyards) and the first tram cars; a fact remembered in a little museum where they keep restored ones and you can take a ride. It also has reconstructions of shops of days gone by. Sir Joseph Paxton, who is best remembered for the Crystal Palace, designed the park in 1843-7, ingeniously converting a swamp by digging lakes into which the water drained, while the soil heaps made pleasant hillocks for planting on. In order to finance it, 100 plots of land were sold for prestige housing to line the circular carriageway running around the outside. It was the first park opened and maintained by a local authority and was copied by many others. Olmsted came to study and make notes before setting out to design Central Park in New York on the same lines.

Many docks are largely silent now and deserve a mention in a book on Hidden Cheshire. No longer bustling, they are quiet havens with views over the sparkling river to Liverpool's imposing sky-line. Birkenhead took over Liverpool's ship building industry from the 1830s. At the time Liverpool was known as the second richest city in the Empire and the wealthy merchants, along with those who travelled from there in the best cabins, were only too glad to see industry removed from the waterfront on that side of the river. It was only as the steam ferries became more reliable that the fabulously well to do chose to move over to this side of the river and build the grand houses which surround Birkenhead, but its middle never achieved the great ideas of a 'city for the future' which were proposed at the start.

To get to Liverpool you can either go through the famous tunnel under the Mersey or take the ferry over it. If you go by boat you can listen to a commentary and the song *Ferry Cross The Mersey* which is a local anthem expressing pride in the district. The first ferry was operated by the monks of Birkenhead Priory which was founded around 1150 by Baron Hamon de Massey. You can find its remains close to the entrance to the tunnel; just a few ruined bits of the monks' dwellings. Their chapter house still functions as a little church for the area and above it the old scriptorium is used as a meeting room and the cloister garden is a place to sit.

BOLLINGTON

Bollington's valley is dominated by mills and White Nancy, looking a bit like an tall igloo. It was built in 1817 to mark the victory at Waterloo and served as a summer house or winter shelter with stone seats around it and a table made from a piece of stone which took eight horses to pull to the summit. The mills made fine textiles using best Egyptian cotton. It is actually in the valley of the Dean which turned the waterwheels in the mills, not the Bollin.

The Dean valley's Bollington is of interest to social historians because Samuel Greg, the son of the founder of Styal Mill, tried to found an ideal workers' colony in the valley. He provided houses with allotments for growing their own vegetables, meetings, Sunday school and evening classes, social facilities and even hot baths, used by men and women on alternative days. His idealism was broken when the workforce, less interested in socialism than decent and reliable wages, went on strike in 1847 during a cotton shortage. Today it still retains its characteristic Pennine appearance with gritstone houses built into the steep valley sides, sometimes one above another in the so called 'stack houses' style where each level has its own entrance.

What looks like a slender watch tower, complete with battlements, is in fact a detached chimney of a mill. In deep valleys the wind was not strong enough for conventional ones, so a tunnel was dug through the stone to emerge higher up and a conventional chimney was added. This took advantage of stronger winds to 'draw' the flame while in the valley there would be days when the smoke would hardly get up a lower chimney.

Following sexual equality laws, one of the old pubs had to change its name. It had been a cattle market where women had not been allowed and was jokingly called 'The Quiet Woman'. When they could no longer be excluded they could no longer be relied upon to stay quiet, so it became 'The Cheshire Hunt'.

BOSTOCK

Bostock is a pretty model village rebuilt towards the end of the 19th century where each house is set in a huge garden so that the tenants could grow their own food. The great house of the France Hayhursts has been restored as expensive apartments and in the grounds is a 17th century half-timbered farmhouse, which was taken down and moved piece by piece from the middle of a car park in the centre of the Lostock chemical works to this more attractive setting in 1998. The Park is private, but the grand house can be seen from the entrance gates, as can a dainty Victorian boat house looking like a setting for an operetta. On the green is a tree grown from an acorn of a much older oak which once grew here. A brass plaque tells us it was planted in 1887 to mark not only Victoria's Golden Jubilee but also Bostock's claim to be at the centre of Cheshire. The county boundaries have been changed many times since, but it is still the spiritual 'heart of the county' - and who on earth can define a real centre of such an amorphous, oddly shaped county to start with?

Peckmill, near the new bypass, was said to be named because the stones were only big enough to grind a peck of corn at a time. It is a pretty building with the mill stream running under it. It is said that the floors were built on many levels to conceal smuggled salt underneath, in the days when there was a heavy tax on salt and Northwich had more Revenue men to collect it than any other similar sized town in England. Almost every farm in Cheshire wanted salt for cheesemaking so there were good profits to be made. At Whatcroft the smugglers used a skeleton which was painted so it glowed in the dark to frighten people away. At Rudheath a tax man was suspicious at the number of funerals there were and opened a coffin to find it full of salt.

BOUGHTON

The road into Chester from the plain goes into a little one-way system as it nears the city. This is Boughton. By the road is a sandstone wall with an inscription to say that it is the burial ground of the hospital of St Giles. This was for lepers and would have been rather like a church, with beds instead of pews. Close to it, St Paul's church was designed by John Douglas - who built his own home on these impressive slopes - to sit on a steep river bank. To keep the weight of the congregation at the end which is most stable he designed it to face south and not east as is normal. The altar part is supported on pillars, and there is a Sunday school underneath in a sort of half cellar. This area is noted for its fine Georgian and Victorian houses.

Behind iron railings overlooking the Dee is the monument to George Marsh who was martyred here for refusing to accept the Catholic religion re-imposed by 'Bloody Mary' in the 16th century. He was one of many who met their ends here. In the end of a row of houses there is a little figure of a man in 17th century dress; who he is and why he is there I am yet to discover.

An unusual feature that might be missed looks rather like a chimney with windows in the side and a lift shaft joined to it. It is the last 'shot tower' in Britain. Lead was heated on the top, after being taken up in the lift, and then when molten it was poured through the floor to drop into a huge tub of water at the bottom. This created perfect spheres for shot. North Wales was a great producer of lead from Roman times and Chester was a centre for making use of it and the silver extracted from it.

BOWDON

This is the superior section of Altrincham, and the two run into each other. Bowdon was an ancient parish, and while much of its church was renewed in the 19th century it keeps a number of monuments from the older church, including one to George Booth. He was the leader of the rebellion in 1659 which intended to bring King Charles II back to the English throne, but ended in defeat at the Battle of Winnington Bridge - the last time that Roundhead and Cavalier were to fight each other. In the 19th century the area was developed for Manchester businessmen who could travel in daily by train but lived on a hill with wide views over Cheshire, well away from the smoke of their factories and the workers' homes. The large mansions which they built are still set in attractive grounds, although many are now too big to be used as single homes. They were just a short carriage ride away from what was tactfully called 'Altrincham and Bowdon Station'. This was served by two types of train. The direct steam train from Chester stopped here and at Sale before going into Manchester, but an electric train ran on a separate line stopping at many stations as it went through Manchester and out to Alderley Edge via Styal, then returned.

Amongst the wealthy who lived in Bowdon was Jesse Hartley, a cotton manufacturer to whom all who are interested in the past owe a great debt. It was he who saved the lovely Ordsall Hall in Salford and gave it to the city to be a museum and social centre. He also sponsored the work of Sir Flinders Petry, the great explorer of Ancient Egypt, who repaid him with finds from his excavations. These he gave to the Manchester University Museum and built an extension to house them. As a result of his generosity Manchester has the finest collection of Egyptology outside London and a collection of world importance.

 ## BRERETON

At the end of a long drive, Brereton Hall and church stand side by side. It is still an imposing house with central turrets joined by a bridge even though parts have been demolished. It was built in 1585 when Margaret Savage came as a bride from the great house at Rock Savage in Runcorn, to remind her of her former home. Rock Savage was destroyed in the Civil War and only bits of the walls remain. The tiny little River Croco runs in front; not far away was its source in the Bagmere. It was said that tree stumps came from the bottom and floated on the surface when a Brereton was due to die - until one tried to cheat death by having the mere drained. You can still see its damp remains in the fields and find its name on OS maps.

The 17th century Bear's Head pub once had a real stuffed bear's head above the door, but the weather has taken its toll. It is not a quaint old village inn any more, being so close to the M6 it has full motel facilities behind. The name comes from a story that a Brereton killed a servant but went to the King to plead for his life. He was imprisoned in the Tower of London with the task of inventing a muzzle for a bear or facing the block. He succeeded and the bear's head with the muzzle became their crest.

THE BRIDESTONES

High in the hills between Leek and Congleton where Neolithic traders crossed between the Dane and the Churnet valleys carrying their coracles on their backs and their stock of stone axes in a bag, is a tomb of Irish style. It shows that people came this way with the knowledge of how it should be built, probably coming through the Mersey and into the Weaver and Dane before using this short route over dry land to the Churnet and the Trent. It is believed the outer chamber was where bodies rested before the cremation and then ashes were passed into the sanctity of the inner chamber through the hole, as if returning to the womb of mother earth. It was once covered by a huge mound of stones and would have been used for centuries.

The hole faces to the west, the place of death and the setting sun, but twice a year the rising male sun god's rays would penetrate the portal as it did at Stonehenge, Abu Simbal and a myriad of other Christian and pagan places of worship. Much later the idea of birth and death was still remembered and newly wed brides - hence The Bridestones - would come to clamber through the 'porthole' to ensure that they had children, sometimes returning again and again if children did not arrive. Such traditions are associated with other holed stones in various parts of the country, always representing birth, and it might have been to stop such superstitious beliefs that the hole was broken. The road between Congleton and Leek passes close to it and it has wonderful views over the Cheshire plain. It is only just in Cheshire by a few steps, the little lane that leads to it follows the county boundary.

BRIMSTAGE

—— Not much of the old Hall remains, but it has been maintained - as so much around here - by the good sense of Lord Leverhulme. The Hall and its former farmyard outbuildings are a pleasant centre selling craftsy things. There is a stairway tower which once gave access to a further floor, long since demolished. In the basement of what was a much larger tower there is a vaulted chamber which may have served as a chapel. Sir Hugh Hulse was given a licence to maintain an oratory in 1398, however it seems strangely big considering that the only other accommodation was two rooms of the same size on top of it - perhaps there were more rooms in timber which have long gone. In one corner the vault is supported by a strange animal. It may be supposed to be a lion but it is one contender for the original grinning Cheshire Cat (see Grappenhall and Pott Shrigley entries). It is now whitewashed, but must have originally been just red stone as it gave the village a pub name: the Red Cat was demolished in 1932. Perhaps he is smiling because he knows the real story but is not telling!

BROMBOROUGH

—— Bromborough is no longer a village but a built up residential area. It is one of a number of places which has been identified with the site of the Battle of Brunabargh, which took place in AD 937 according to the *Anglo Saxon Chronicle*. A confederation of Norsemen, Welsh and Scots stood against the English King Athelstan but were defeated. There are Saxon remains, just. A couple of fragments of crosses are preserved in the church which is Victorian but stands on a place where worship has taken place since Saxon times.

Social historians will search out the houses of Bromborough Pool. They were built for the workers of Price's Candle Works in the 1850s and are one of the Victorian model factory villages of which Port Sunlight, only a mile away, is the best known. The term is used in the same sense as an artist's model, as something to be copied, rather than a miniature. There were allotments, a village hall and its own school. Almost revolutionary in their time, the houses actually had indoor flushing lavatories.

BRUERA

A pretty village on the Westminster Estate with houses typical of those designed for it by John Douglas. The church is much older than its surroundings with a Norman chancel arch. In the churchyard there is what some writers have described as a 'circle' of yew trees, suggesting that this indicates a much older religious significance, a sort of growing version of Stonehenge, inside which the church was built. However, closer examination shows the shape to be a rectangle and the trees are not big enough to be older than the church. It remains a pretty spot, even if not pagan, and around the farm opposite are the dry remains of a moat. Close by is Saighton Grange, one of the country homes of the Abbot of Chester, but very much altered in Victorian times and now used as a school.

BUNBURY

Oscar Wilde's 'Ernest' invented a friend called Bunbury to explain his visits to the country, but you will need no excuse to seek out the church at Bunbury, on a little knoll. It is one of the most visited in Cheshire. Inside is the monumental effigy to Hugh Calveley, a contemporary of the Black Prince, with three calves on his surcoat - a punning reference to his name known to students of heraldry as a 'rebus'. He rebuilt the church to be a college where several priests would pray for his soul and the black and white College House where they lived is in the valley below the churchyard by a narrow deeply cut road. Both have been much altered since his day. Other men of valour depicted on their tombs are George Beeston, shown wearing the armour in which he fought against the Spanish Armada when he was 89, and Ralph Egerton, standard bearer to Henry VIII.

My favourite monument stands by the 1663 font in a corner at the back, as if in disgrace. Jane Johnson of Nantwich wears a fashionable low cut dress of the 18th century She was once placed by the side of the communion table at the front but a Victorian vicar found the low cut dress and 'bulging udders' too offensive, especially for the choirboys to see when their minds should have been on other things. The monument was buried in the churchyard, until dug up some years later, when another vicar pronounced it was a rare and ancient statue of the Virgin as she was holding a dove. What he made of the neckline is not recorded!

The church was damaged during the Second World War. German bombers returning from raids on Liverpool would unload any remaining bombs on Cheshire to make their planes lighter to save fuel on returning and make crash landings less hazardous. While the church was being restored after the war it received an unusual gift. Curtains on the doors were made from fabric which had been specially woven in silver and blue and used in Westminster Abbey as part of the decoration for the Coronation in 1953.

Bunbury village has old cottages and a corner shop with a figure of a Scotsman in a kilt smoking a long clay pipe, an old advert for a tobacconist. The large black and white Wild Boar Hotel is a Victorian concoction but the most mysterious structure is a bit further along the road to Whitchurch. A little cottage was said to have been built by a poacher who returned from his seven years hard labour in Australia to claim the land by building a chimney and having it smoking between sunset and sunrise. On the front are carvings of the sheriff and his men; who the poacher cursed. On the top of the wooden columns supporting the porch (originally part of a four poster bed!) are two heads which look as if they may actually be much older 'Celtic heads' of pre-Christian times. Beatrice Tunstall wrote her novel *The Shiny Night* around the story.

BURLEYDAM

Near the Shropshire border, Burleydam has the park of Combermere Abbey with its lake. The Abbey is still a private residence. It was once home to Cistercian monks, and became the home of the Cotton family. The most colourful character in its history was the Empress of Austria who spent two hunting seasons here in the 19th century. She cut a dashing figure in hunting circles and it is recorded that to keep the elegant styles that she admired she was actually sewn into her riding habit each morning.

The Combermere Arms is an old hostelry but the present building is not nearly as old as the Abbey. It is supposed to have a ghost which is kept in a bottle under the front doorstep. This is unlikely enough, but according to the story it is of a monk, who used a secret passage to come from the Abbey for a drink. Secret passage stories exist anywhere that there is something old, and are usually someone's imagination or can be traced to discoveries of drains. In this case the idea of popping underground for a drink would be most unlikely as the monastic rules laid down that every monk should have a gallon of ale a day. Not that this was to encourage drunken behaviour, but there was little else that they could drink as water was likely to be polluted, milk might carry infections, tea and coffee had yet to be introduced and fizzy drinks were unheard of!

BURTON

An old village on the edge of the Dee, Burton was one of those to which ships moved as the sands engulfed the port at Chester, only to be overtaken by the sands itself. Since the Second World War people have come here to attend adult education courses. It was one of the socialist principles that emerged during the war that adults who had never had the chance of higher education because they had to go to work should have the opportunity to learn. Residential colleges were set up in each county, where anyone could go for a weekend and study a new topic. The lectures were delivered by guest professionals, and it gave opportunities for discussion and making friends in attractive settings. Cheshire chose Burton Manor, a splendid sandstone mansion in a pretty village. For many of the first to study here, who had attended elementary schools in industrial towns and gone on to work long hours in factories or to the war, it was a first unbelievable taste of the countryside and of visiting a grand house. Today few are prevented from attending college because of poverty and there are far more university places and so the Manor is as likely to hold high powered management training courses or professional conferences as those providing an understanding of philosophy or how to draw. People are welcome to visit the gardens and admire the views of the Welsh Mountains over the Dee but report to the office first for security reasons.

Burton Wood (not to be confused with the Warrington

brewery) is a National Trust property and in Station Road is a little garden where plaques on stone columns resting on the ground tell you about St Patrick's Well, which later became known as Hampston's Well. It was the main water supply and people were prohibited from taking their washing to it as this would pollute it - they had to take the water home.

The church is mainly of 1721 with a one-fingered clock on the tower and an interesting box on the north wall which once contained a chained Bible. It has long been missing, but the box is a unique survival in the county of the days when Puritan ideals encouraged people to go into the church and read the Bible for themselves. By the churchyard wall is a little fenced off area with a plaque telling of two mysterious gravestones said to mark the last resting place of two Quakers who would not be buried in consecrated ground. It seems rather unlikely that if they were so averse to consecrated ground (as all Quakers were) they would have been buried so close to it. It is an old tradition and the only alternative - that they were old stones thrown out of the churchyard - seems like heresy. One day perhaps the chance to see who is or is not under them will arise and it would not be the first empty grave in Burton (look under Puddington for the story of Father Pleasington).

🌿 BURTONWOOD

North of Warrington was the biggest American air base in Britain from which wartime bombers flew and where servicemen were based during the long years after VE and VJ Day which we remember as the 'Cold War'. It is easy to see why they were based here for Cheshire is just about at the centre of mainland Britain - although it has its coastline, Wales and Cornwall jut further west and it is roughly half way down the map of England and Scotland. Indeed, when Warrington New Town Corporation advertised for new businesses to move there it always claimed to be at the centre of Britain. If you look at the layout of the Ordnance Survey 'Pathfinder' series you will see how the maps for the rest of Britain all expand from a place called Greenhill at Whitley, south of Warrington. It is the only junction of four maps to form a perfect cross in the whole country without overlapping.

From Warrington no one defending Europe could be sure

which way the planes would fly or troops would set out. It was just as far to go to Scotland or Cornwall or any point in between while those defending Europe had to watch the coasts from Spain to Norway for possible invasion. During and just after the Second World War over 3,000 local girls left this area to become GI brides and settle in America. After the war the County Council decided to send 1,000 mixed race babies who had been born out of wedlock locally, to be adopted by Afro-American families rather than live in orphanages in this country. Today such things are only fading memories and Burtonwood is best known for its ale which is much appreciated by the members of CAMRA and those who just enjoy a good pint. The old air base is now an industrial estate. The days when entertainers like Bing Crosby and Bob Hope came to entertain the troops are just a memory - but as the song says 'Thanks for the memory'.

CALDY

———— Pevsner in *The Buildings of England* says of Caldy, 'Cheshire is something of a Surrey of the North, but Surrey has nothing to compare with this'. Its old manor was taken over by Richard Watson Barton in 1832. He was one of a number of Manchester merchants who settled in the Wirral. His son continued the transformation of the village then it passed to Alexander Eccles, a Liverpool cotton broker. In 1906 the estate was split into housing development plots. The smallest was an acre and this influenced the sort of houses built during the Edwardian period, in the very last years of big house building. After the First World War fashions changed and with servants in short supply no one wanted to build so sumptuously any more. Some are now split into apartments but the village remains as a glimpse of Edwardian elegance.

CAPESTHORNE

———— One of Cheshire's grand houses with a front longer than Buckingham Palace is the home of the Bromley Davenport family. It contains many treasures including ancient Greek pottery and furniture from America, besides the famous

The Pepper Pot Lodge at Capesthorne Hall

'Paradise Bed' embroidered for Bramall Hall by Dame Dorothy Davenport. She filled the bed hangings with scenes of Adam and Eve in the garden of Eden, a bit saucy for bed covers it must be said with its tale of 'original sin'. However, the house is not the subject here, but the lodge. Copied from the Elizabethan-style turrets on the main house it, like the house, was designed by Blore and built between 1837-9. Because of its shape it was soon nicknamed the Pepper Pot Lodge. It has three square floors with a roof which is shaped so that the whole structure resembles a pepper pot. At the time that it was built salt was not served from this shaped container, but from little glass dishes or glass-lined silver containers using tiny spoons. Until the 20th century when the modern method of manufacturing salt in a vacuum was invented, all salt crystals were tiny cubes and would jam together in a modern pourer. It seems appropriate in Cheshire, so well known for salt, that we should savour it with a bit of pepper and a tale of salt cellars past.

CARDEN

A pair of sandstone lodges with elaborate gates between, through which you can watch a herd of deer, mark the entrance to Carden Park. The lodges have decorative chimney pots in the shape of Classical urns! The hall burnt down in 1912, but there has been a luxury hotel, golf and leisure development there which includes the most northerly vineyard in Europe making its own wine.

John Harris occupied a cave in the park for 20 years during the 19th century. At that time it was fashionable for the best mansions to employ a hermit to wander about the grounds with unkempt hair and uncut fingernails; they were paid not to talk to anyone. Carden's was a bit more fussy than most, having come from a well to do family, insisting on a servant and that they both had feather beds. As fashions changed and hermits were no longer 'in', he moved into what was known as Allenscomb's Cave, near to what is now the Sandstone Trail; its modern name, altered from the original to 'Mad Allan's Hole', can still be seen on the OS maps.

The old mill of the Carden estate, at Stretton, was rescued by the County Council and has been restored to working order, so on certain days you can go to see the process of grinding flour. Unusually, the mill has two types of water wheel to operate when the water in the pool is at differing levels.

CARRINGTON

This was once a mossland and too dangerous to cross, but it provided a novel answer to some of Manchester's most unpleasant problems in the 19th century. In the days before proper sewerage was provided there had to be some way of getting rid of the waste from hundreds of thousands of buckets which were used in simple privies. There were also the ashes from hundreds of hearths - and the Duke of Bridgewater's canal provided the answer. Special barges were used to bring the contents of the privies, horse and other muck from the streets and the ashes from the fires. The ashes were used to support railway lines over the moss and the waste was dumped to the side. Eventually nature did the rest, breaking it down to form excellent soil which was ideal for farming and for market gardening to supply the people living in the towns.

Today the results of all this have a far more glamorous use. The magnificent training facilities of Manchester United Football Club are built on it! The ultra modern building and first rate exercise grounds are masked behind trees but let us hope that the origins of the ground on which they play has the same good effect on the game that it had on the crops planted upon it!

 ## CHECKLEY

There is not much to Checkley and never was, but it almost became the great crossroads of the early Industrial Revolution in a forgotten story kept only in the archives of the Weaver Navigation's early years. The Act to allow the river to be made navigable was passed in 1721 and by the 1730s there was a flourishing trade developing with a wharf at Winsford from which goods were carried by packhorse to the Potteries and even on to Derby. Mainly it was china clay which came one way and finished pots which were sent for export via Liverpool.

Then in the 1750s the idea of a canal to join the Weaver and the Humber, and to link with others to the Thames and Severn, was devised. Not wanting their river to be sidelined those responsible for the Weaver Navigation offered to extend their navigable waterway to Checkley along the little brook. They were only empowered to improve the existing rivers and brooks and had to keep within the county of Chester. They felt that they could improve Checkley Brook, just as the Sankey Brook had been developed, and keep within the law. It would then be up to the other companies to make their links to Checkley. Unfortunately the subsidence, which was to cause such problems in Northwich, had started to show and Josiah Wedgwood decided that it would be best to take the Trent and Mersey direct to Runcorn and not to join the Weaver. So Checkley never became a canal terminal. In the 19th century there were plans to revive the idea with a ship canal to go to Stoke and Birmingham along the route. This came as a response to the railways which were building side-lines to the salt works in the 1870s and taking away the river trade but, alas, it was never started.

Not far from Checkley we find Betley Mere. The county

boundaries have changed since Fletcher Moss in his 1901 volume of *Pilgrimages to Old Homes* wrote of it that it is in two counties, two parishes, two deaneries, two dioceses and two archbishoprics. Presumably all that was too much for local government to cope with so a slight kink was put in the county boundary to put it all in Staffordshire or it would also be in two boroughs today. I guess the church boundaries are still the same as they were, for the diocese of Chester is the same plan as the pre-1974 county boundary, so it deserves a mention here. Even if it is not, Betley itself is an attractive Staffordshire village, worth the effort of crossing so many boundaries to see.

CHESTER

The Cathedral is the third most visited cathedral in Britain, partly because Chester is on the international tourist trail for people who come to England through Manchester Airport, visit Liverpool for its Beatles associations, 'do Chester' in a couple of hours then are on their way to Stratford on Avon and London.

For those who can spend time and linger in what a 19th century writer called 'the most romantic city in the world', there are many hidden corners. That description needs explaining today, for modern minds think it implies somewhere to fall in love or spend your honeymoon. In fact it refers to the Romantic movement in art which pictured things in the past as if in a Gothic novel - 'Romance' in French. Road widening, building improvements, new shops and even the advent of pedestrianisation have changed the face of the city for ever, and not necessarily for the better. Its crowds of tourists sounding like those on the Tower of Babel, speaking many tongues, also obscure that which they have come to see by their very numbers. It is better to visit 'out of season'.

There are a few curious things in the Cathedral which might be missed. One, a tiny painting of the Virgin and Child which was supposedly painted on fabric made from spiders' webs; it is actually very fine silk and is on show in the corner of the north transept. Under one of the carved misericord seats in the choir you will need to search to find St Werburgh and the geese, or even ask a verger to show you. The story is that the geese agreed only to graze their allotted parts if no one hunted them. This was respected for a time until one was shot. The geese went to complain to the Saint, who found the culprit had already cooked the goose. However, when she prayed the bird rose from the pot - and all lived happily ever after. You can see her shrine, carefully restored, in the Lady Chapel behind the altar, with niches in the side for the heads of praying pilgrims.

Amongst numerous other stories I might single out the elephant carved with horses' hooves. There was no zoo for 14th century carvers to go and study so this one based it on the biggest thing he had seen - the ancestor of a shire horse. It deserves mention because the original 'elephant and castle' was not an Indian one with a howdah, but derived from the wife of Edward I when people could not get their tongues round her Spanish title of Infanta de Castile. You may think that all is ancient in the Cathedral, but on the south transept you will find carvings included when it was restored in Victorian times. There you will find animals with satirical heads - Mr Gladstone is undermining emblems of the Pope and Mr Disraeli defending a crown (though it is not actually the crown of England!) against a beast with the cap of liberty, which was the emblem of the French Revolution.

If you look over the road from the door at the end of the long south transept you will see what looks like a church used as a shop. It was, indeed, a church. When the abbey needed to extend its provision of altars in the 14th century, as each priest needed to say mass each day, the only way they could build was south but the church of St Oswald was in the way. The parishioners agreed to move to a new church that the monks would build for them, which they did. However, when the transept was complete they decided they wanted to move back and abandoned the church, which has been used for many things from a skating rink to a theatre in the past; in fact everything but a church!

Most of Chester's apparently ancient half-timbered buildings are in fact Victorian and were designed in the era of romantic revivals. Chester has plenty of romantic tales in the Victorian sense. Like the little Pepper Gate by the huge New Gate through which the daughter of the Mayor eloped to Wales. It was kept locked afterwards, giving the saying 'locking the Pepper Gate after the daughter is stolen'. Find God's Providence House in Watergate Street where the inscription 'God's providence is mine inheritance' is said to record that it was the only house in the city to escape the plague - because it had a bunch of onions on the door. The structure is a Victorian reconstruction, done for the Archaeology Society to show how half -timbered buildings could be built, but it is not in local vernacular tradition. Look also for the Old Leche House near it, the home of the Leches of Carden, now an antiques shop. If you peep through the window you will see the strange 'cage' with bars through which people upstairs could see downstairs without being seen themselves.

Chester was the Roman fortress of Deva and the north walls still stand higher than any other Roman fortress walls anywhere. The rest have been renewed over the years and to the south and east the city has been extended to enclose more land. Where the ditch once was by the North Wall, is now the canal with the little 'bridge of sighs', between the former Northgate Prison and the chapel in the Bluecoat Hospital - where condemned men were taken to say their last prayers. Nothing like as grand as the one in Venice, but incredibly narrow. The Hospital is now used as the History Department of Chester College, and through the arch under a statue of a bluecoat boy you can see a lovely little courtyard. Can there be a more appropriate place to study the past?

Over the old Dee Bridge in Handbridge is a unique little shrine with a statue of Minerva, the goddess of wisdom and patron of quarrymen, carved in the rock in the quarries where the Romans dug their sandstone. It is called Edgar's Field as the Saxon King was rowed on the Dee by six subjected princes. They had refused to attend his coronation in London, but he travelled to Chester, at the edge of his kingdom, to receive homage from the King of Scotland, the Prince of Wales and the Viking rulers of the Isle of Man and other islands. Chester was a major port for trade with Ireland until the 16th century and if you are lucky enough to see the Lord Mayor in procession you will see that in front of him is carried the usual mace and a silver oar, for he still holds the title 'Admiral of the Dee' long after that river's trade moved to the Mersey. You can see a portrayal of Edgar and his princes in stained glass in St John's church where there is a most bizarre monument to Diana Warburton who died in 1693. No portrait here but a full size anatomically correct standing skeleton holding a shroud, with three skulls on the front of a black marble table. Such monuments were intended to remind everyone that they would end up in the grave, but Christians could be assured of resurrection. They were not morbid to contemporary eyes but intended to remind you that the soul would live on after the body went to the grave. There are also parts of 'wheel headed crosses' which were set up by Norse settlers who lived around the church of St Olave (Olaf). Not all Vikings raided and pillaged. These were allowed to settle as traders, here outside the ruined Roman walls and in the Wirral, on condition that they did not cause problems for the rest of Mercia.

Below it, now on the edge of a bowling green, can be seen the Hermitage. Legend tells how King Harold did not die at Hastings, but came to spend his last days there. The origin of the name actually has more to do with the Hermitage in St Petersburg, that is a place to escape from the troubles of the world, rather than to do with religious men, royal or otherwise, who lived alone. The building is part of a much later house pretending to be older than it is and was the childhood home of the writer De Quincey (1785-1859). He joined the nature loving community of the Lake District poets, but ever eager to experience more he was one of the many intellectuals of the period to try using narcotic drugs. He wrote it all down in a book called *Confessions of an Opium Eater*, which inspired the early 'hippies' of the 1960s who would read it avidly.

Follow the Walls until you are above the grandstand on the racecourse (the oldest in Britain) and look down. The stonework you see behind is the remains of the Roman wharf; for what is now the track was then all water where ships came. Look in the middle and you will see a little stump of a stone cross which gave the place its name. It was the Rood Eye - nothing to do with peeping Toms but the Island of the Cross. It is said to mark the place where a miracle was once believed to have happened. A wooden statue of the Virgin was found washed up on the island. People felt it was a divine sign and flocked to see it, until the truth emerged. It had stood in the church in Hawarden until it fell and killed a woman. In the Middle Ages animals and even statues which killed someone had to be punished. They decided they could not hang her as it would be sacrilege and so put her in the Dee and she floated to Chester. If that is not curiosity enough, look behind over the road and find a porch with two doors, the last sedan chair porch in the city. The occupant could get in under cover while the porters stood outside the two doors.

CHRISTLETON

Not far from Chester, with pretty views of the pool with its wild fowl, which was created from old clay-pits needed for brickmaking works. Now it is overlooked by a charming row of timbered almshouses. The church is by a little green with the parish pump and an odd little shelter which looks as if someone forgot to put the seats in it. In the churchyard near the path is a stone to William Huggins, a Liverpool artist who specialised in animal pictures drawn from life. He only spent the last four years of his life in Christleton and by then was virtually retired and unable to paint because of arthritis. Christleton Hall is now used as a college for training in the law.

By the A41, people often remark on what looks like a rather out-grown dovecote standing high above the traffic. It 'stands out like a sore thumb' but deserves a place in this book because hardly anyone would guess what it is for. In fact it is a pump which moves the sewage from Christleton over a slight hill and into the Chester sewage treatment system!

CHURCH LAWTON

In days gone by unmarried girls who found that they were expecting a baby would leave their village and often ended up going to London where they would abandon the child at a workhouse. Girls who mysteriously vanished were said to have 'given Lawton Gate a slam', as the main road to London passed that way. It has a church with a Norman arch, though most of the rest has been renewed, and which keeps memories of a violent thunderstorm in 1652. The congregation was so full that some were sitting in the bell-tower and felt the full force of the lightning. The vicar calmed his congregation and carried on until the end of the service before he discovered that eleven men and boys were dead.

CHURCH MINSHULL

This is one of the prettiest little villages with half-timbered houses, one with an unusual projecting room above the door which forms a sort of porch. Only a lucky change in national politics saved the village, for in the 1960s there were plans to build a new city, a Milton Keynes of the North, which would have completely surrounded it but with a change of government the idea was abandoned. An important feature is a little retaining wall in front of some cottage gardens which is made of clinker bass, which was the residue from burning poor quality coal in Winsford's salt works. This is one of the very last examples of its use as a building material - it resembles a black stone sponge.

On the outside wall of the church is a monument with a memory of the dispute over the Gawsworth inheritance which caused a duel in which Lord Mohun and the Duke of Hamilton killed each other. The story starts in Gawsworth where the church contains a monument to Sir Edward Fitton, who died in 1643, showing his only daughter who died as a child before him. Fitton's sisters both laid their claim to the estates when he died, although he had said that he would rather leave everything to the Parish Beadle than let either of them have a penny. There were law suits, fraudulent wills and the arguments went on with accusations and ill feelings for years. Eventually the representatives of the two sides met in a London park at dawn. It was the only duel in English history in which both parties died. This monument was set up by the family of Thomas Minshull, whose mother, as the inscription records, 'was one of Sir Edward's sisters who had suffered great wrongs by unjust people'.

Lovers of *The Wind in the Willows* will be delighted to know that the village has its own Toad Hall, a splendid 17th century timber-framed house once belonging to the miller and backing onto the river near the old water mill. The wheel was converted to provide the village's own electricity supply which it did until the 1950s. On the other side of the road a more modern house keeps up the fun with the name Frog Manor. It is a bore to say there are several others in the north and that it is actually T'owd Hall (the old hall). Sit by the gentle waters of the Weaver amongst the willows and pretend...

CODDINGTON

Coddington is a strange village with its church, mill, smithy, village hall and old farmhouses all arranged around the 'Mudfield'. Perhaps it was once the 'Moundfield' as it has a mound with Scots firs, which is a mystery. It has been claimed to be many things including a Bronze Age or Saxon burial mound, a windmill hill or even a small Norman castle. It is probably a burial mound of some date, but so far no definite answer has been found.

CONGLETON

Congleton Rare, Congleton Rare,
Sold the Church Bible to buy a bear.

The story is that the old bear had died just before the Wakes and the town purchased a new one by using the money that had been collected to buy a Bible. In the 17th century this action would have been even more provocative than it is today, for the Puritans tried to prevent bear baiting and all sports, preferring people to spend their time reading the Bible. It was interpreted by contemporaries that they had turned their back on religion and taken to sport instead - an act practically akin to selling their souls to the Devil. Congleton still likes its fun and holds what is claimed to be the biggest carnival in England every summer.

Congleton was a silk making town. In the past industry was far more governed by climate than it is today and the slight differences between west Cheshire and west Lancashire made Cheshire better for silk and Lancashire ideal for cotton. There are cottages with a third floor with extra wide windows to be seen in several streets. They were built to give light to hand looms which would weave silk in the 18th and 19th centuries. The River Dane provided power to turn water wheels which drove the 'throwing' (the correct word for spinning silk) machines and there are still some fine mills in the town, though they no longer throw silk.

In a book on hidden things it is appropriate to remember two important hoards found in Congleton. Three large dark glazed pots full of silver coins were found which had been hidden during the Civil War; it was the biggest hoard of its type found in the county. A hoard of another kind was of broken weapons and bronze which had been buried by a trader in the Bronze Age. This is known as a founder's hoard, because it was probably left by a bronzesmith, who no doubt intended to make use of the metal but never got round to it.

Its church used to be one of the most interesting in Cheshire to students of the history of worship, for it retained a 17th century pulpit in the middle of its 18th century nave - the only church in the diocese to do so. In the 18th century the long sermon was by far the most important part of the service and huge pulpits, high enough to see into the galleries, were provided in all churches right in the centre. However, when I took a party of students to view, it had gone. Victim of modern videos of weddings. The brides did not like it obscuring the cameraman's view of their vows at the altar! They sold the Bible to buy a bear and got rid of the pulpit to satisfy wedding fashions - a rare town indeed. A second stanza could be added to the rhyme to say:

Now Congleton Pride, Congleton Pride,
Got rid of their pulpit to video the bride.

CREWE

Crewe is at the hub of the railway system. Even its coat of arms has an iron wheel at the centre with the spokes representing the railway lines which meet here. There was no town of Crewe until the 1840s when side-lines to Chester and Manchester were needed as branches from the original 1837 railway line which George Stephenson engineered between London and Glasgow. Today they call it the West Coast Line, although it rarely gets near the coast. It is a tradition that Nantwich and Winsford refused to allow the junction because of the smoke so a 'greenfields site' was developed. Strangely the station is on the edge of town, and not in the middle as they did not want to add smoke from the trains to that from the chimneys of the houses and the locomotive works. An old saying tells 'that which is not Crewe is Crewe but that which is Crewe is not Crewe' and dates from the days when the station was actually outside the Borough. The first town was designed by Joseph

Lock, although not much of his original structure remains. The substantial mid-Victorian houses each have a porch and in many there are panels of Victorian 'self cleaning tiles'. They were made in Stoke and include floral designs as well as figures and birds - a lovely gallery of Victorian taste for all to admire.

The Town Hall, part of an Edwardian group along with the market and a delightful theatre, has two weather vanes, one in the form of Stephenson's Rocket and the other a Rolls-Royce car, for they too are made in Crewe. A further transport landmark is recalled by the Merlin pub. It has nothing to do with birds of prey or magicians but was the name of the engine of the wartime Spitfires which were made at the Rolls-Royce factory.

A special orchard dedicated to saving examples of old Cheshire fruit is preserved in the University campus which was built away from the town surrounded by fields. In case these are damaged in any way the Earl of Chester, Prince Charles, has agreed to keep duplicate specimens in his grounds at Highgrove in Gloucestershire so that there is more than one 'stock', but far enough apart to prevent cross infections. Perhaps it is not so unexpected for the Borough regularly comes top in the Britain in Bloom Contest.

 ## CREWE GREEN

—— There are actually two Crewes, one each side of the station (not to mention a third village with the same name near the Dee). Crewe Green is a delightful model village built for tenants of the Earl of Crewe. Crewe Hall was one of the biggest Elizabethan houses in Cheshire. It was largely rebuilt after a fire in the 19th century to be as near to the original as possible and is now a hotel. Amongst the picturesque cottages is a little church where the first vicar, John Ellerton, wrote the hymn *The day though gavest Lord is ended* in 1870. Moved by lines such as 'o'er each continent and island' and 'like earth's proud empires,' the head of the largest Empire the world has ever known was impressed by the theme of Christian unity under the sun which never set on her Empire. Queen Victoria chose it to be sung throughout the Empire on Diamond Jubilee Day in 1897. On a plaque on the front of the little school you see Father Time rewarding a good student with a book and a laurel wreath as

Crewe Green school

prizes with one hand and whipping a lazy pupil with the other. School could be hard in those days!

DARESBURY

It is pronounced with the 'a' as in car, and can be seen from a long way away because of the huge tower of the Daresbury laboratories, which contain a Van Der Graaf generator. Modern though it looks science has moved on so it is obsolete and it is now an antiquity in its own right. It is in an independent facility which carries out work for universities and government agencies.

The village is well known for its links with Lewis Carroll, who was born Charles Lutwidge Dodgson here. Who better to include in a book about the curious than the man who made the Cheshire Cat famous. The writer was a brilliant mathematician and Oxford don but found it easier to communicate with children. The Dodo is believed to be a joke against himself stammering to say his name. There is not much that you can find that is definitely associated with him. The church where his father was parson (the village never had a vicar) was rebuilt after his time, but contains the famous memorial stained glass window. There is some old woodwork and a Jacobean pulpit but little else that he would remember. His birthplace has also gone, but the site has been excavated and is marked by a memorial stone. Long after he left he wrote:

> I watch the drowsy night expire
> And fancy paints at my desire
> Her magic pictures in the fire,
> An island farm midst seas of corn
> Swayed by the blessed breath of morn,
> The happy place where I was born.

There is a former Sessions House of 1841 in the village with a Latin inscription on the front which it is hoped will one day hold a Lewis Carroll exhibition though it is now part of the pub and has a mural of the Mad Hatter's tea party inside.

DARNHALL

Its very name means hidden hole, as in the word darning for hiding a hole in a sock, so assures it of a place here. There is not much to see, a view from a bridge in a narrow piece of road, too dangerous to stop. Instead park by the little village hall with its traditional red telephone box and walk down. There is an old mill on a site going back to the Middle Ages, when there was a corn mill and a fulling mill to process new cloth. Now all is peaceful here amidst the trees but it has many memories of violence.

This was the site of the hunting lodge of the Norman Earls of Chester where wild boar and deer were hunted. While staying here with his wife, Helen (the daughter of Llewellyn the Prince of Wales and granddaughter of King John), Earl John le Scot was found dead. The rumours started that Helen had poisoned him but nothing could be proved. The Norman earls of Chester made their own laws as William the Conqueror had given Cheshire a status making it almost a separate state within a state. Then

Henry III took Cheshire in hand and eventually made his son Edward Earl of Chester; a title always since then held by the oldest son of a monarch. Edward intended to build an abbey here, but the monks asked to be moved to what became Vale Royal and simply kept a grange farm here.

In the Middle Ages there were disputes about fishing here between the Abbot and the Venables family, Barons of Kinderton, which often turned violent. The abbey ledger book is full of complaints. At the time the Darnhall peasants staged a revolt, asking the King for better rights and when they did not get them the Abbot's 'servant' John de Bodeworth was shot in an ambush by the peasants, led by a Venables. The killers cut off his head then kicked it like a ball. Often people have portrayed the peasants as downtrodden men simply asking for 'human rights' against cruel oppression. It is an idea which suits modern ideals. In fact closer study of the documents reveals that the uprising at Darnhall coincided exactly with the Venables' dispute. The implication is that they encouraged the violence for their own ends in the legal wrangle over fishing in the pool. There were still extensive pools behind the weir filled with fish until the 1960s when the fish were netted and moved to other pools before the weir was demolished. Then a prophesy of Robert Nixon, the ploughboy of Over, came true. He said Darnhall Pool would become a lane, and there is a cattle track through it today.

In 1828 poachers surrounded the Hall at Christmas time taking pot shots at the gamekeeper and servants and killing every pheasant in sight. They were apprehended and found guilty of carrying guns by night, a devious way of using the law passed to prevent rebellions rather than arouse more anger by charging them with poaching. They were actually on the ship ready for transportation to Australia when a canny lawyer noted that although the witnesses had said they were seen around 12 o'clock none had said if it was noon or night. The old Hall has long been demolished; but 'The Knobs' remain. They were former gateposts moved to the sides of the road when it was widened.

In the woods is hidden one of the outlying radio dishes operated from Jodrell Bank. You can see it from a distance but within a few yards it is totally obscured by the trees. To build a replacement for the 'big dish' at Jodrell would have cost too much and been almost impossible to operate. Instead, a group of seven small dishes were built in the early 1980s, so that signals from all could be used together to create a 'multiple dish interferometer', which allows distant parts of the universe to be studied. Hidden in these Cheshire lanes, the origins of time are being unravelled.

DELAMERE FOREST

Large parts of the forest have recently been flooded to recreate a mossland. That is the way much of the forest would actually have looked before it was drained, between the wars, then planted with numerous straight conifers which were destined for pit props. Now the coal pits have gone and props are no longer needed, more varied landscapes are being introduced. Today large areas are planted for a variety of Christmas trees. At one time the forest trees were not suitable, but to prevent people from destroying saplings they imported trees from Wales to sell here. Now you can select your own as it is growing in the autumn and collect it ready prepared in December. There are also growing areas where half the new trees which are planted in Britain's forests start their life, so as old trees are felled new ones are ready to take their place. You can find out more about the natural history in a little museum near the railway station, where you can buy maps showing the best ways to walk in the forest and find its hidden places. Many visitors do not go far from the roads which are often lined with cars, but there are quiet paths to explore.

Delamere has a long history and gained its forest title as the Earl of Chester was the eldest son of the monarch and only a royal hunting area could be termed forest - a legal term which actually need not imply trees at all. James I enjoyed hunting there when he visited but in the time of Charles II it was decided that as they were no longer hunted by royalty the deer should all be slaughtered. Delamere's royal associations are still marked by the royal coat of arms, insignia and date on houses within its former bounds though most was enclosed from 1812 when all the roads were straightened. This gave rise to a particularly straight section of the main road to Winsford and Middlewich that started an idea that it was Roman. In fact it is just like all other roads in the forest, none have bends but as a main road this tends to stand out on maps. The church dates from 1816. Before then the forest was extra-parochial - that is, without a church. Because it was not a parish, many unmarried mothers fled to the forest to avoid the hardships of the workhouse. Lord Delamere paid for a 'soop kitchen' to feed them in the 1840s when workhouses were at their worst. After the victory at Waterloo the Government set aside money to provide churches where they were needed and this was a Waterloo Church.

DISLEY

The village is at the entrance to Lyme Park, which doubled as Mr Darcy's house in the television adaptation of *Pride and Prejudice* and this was the very lake in which he swam in an often repeated scene. High on the moors overlooking the National Trust's magnificent house and park are the Bow Stones, sections of round shafted crosses in the Norse style of late Saxon date. In the grounds is the grim looking Cage, which was actually intended to be used to watch events in the park from the top while food was prepared and where guests could sleep overnight. If this seems a bit extravagant for watching hunting and races compare it to the best of modern hospitality suites at the racecourses.

They used to count the deer in the park each year when they were forced to cross a lake, an event recalled in plaster work around a wall in one of the rooms in the hall. In the church is the grave of Joseph Watson who died at the age of 104 in 1753, having been gamekeeper to five generations and his grave records that he was the first to 'perfect ye art of driving ye stags'. This was slightly different for it actually refers to his ability to drive a herd of them where he wanted them to go. He won a bet for one of the Leghs by delivering a small herd to Windsor Castle without one loss.

DODDINGTON

Not far away is Bridgemere Garden World, the largest such complex in the country and a Mecca for garden enthusiasts which even has its own television series offering gardening tips.

Doddington Park was set out by our most famous gardener, 'Capability Brown', and the road passes the lake where Canada geese swim amongst the sailboats. The house and grounds are private, but glimpsed from the road is a strange little fortified tower. It is basically a north country 'tower house' and a 'licence to crenelate' (put battlements on it) was given in the 14th century. It has a strange stairway in front, of 17th century style, with statues of the Black Prince and the four Cheshire squires who distinguished themselves at the Battle of Poitiers in 1356.

That came from the old hall which was demolished in the 1770s to be replaced by a splendid Wyatt building, which you can see peeping through the trees. A 20th century African mystery is recalled here. Sir Henry John Delves Broughton, the last of the family, married and left to start a new life in Kenya away from the threats of Hitler's impending war. They became involved in the scandalous case featured in the book and film *White Mischief* which exposed the lives of rich and decadent English people who had taken refuge in Kenya rather than serve their country. Although acquitted of the murder of Lord Erroll, Broughton committed suicide in Liverpool's Adelphi Hotel and took the real truth of who was guilty (if he ever knew) to his grave.

DODLESTON

There is a tiny part of Cheshire which extends to the west of the Dee and was used by the Normans to prevent the Welsh getting too close to the walls of Chester when they built castles at Pulford and Dodleston. Now Chester has expanded over much of it. Television cameras were to be seen in a field in Poulton recently following the excavation of a small monastic cell. It was originally founded for Cistercian monks to pray for the safety of the Earl of Chester by his baker when he was a prisoner of King Stephen in 1153. Because of Welsh raids the monks moved to Dieulacres in Staffordshire. The manor of Dodleston passed to the Manleys but attention was aroused when it was possible to link them to a family now living in Dorset. A facial reconstruction from a skeleton found on the site, paid for by the television company, showed remarkable similarity to the present Mr Manley. The bones were buried again and what is left of the chapel is under a field at the end of the little country lane.

The home of the Manleys was at Dodleston Hall and was garrisoned by Sir William Brereton during the siege of Chester and the Dodleston church registers record the burial of Royalists executed by his men. The church, which has been rebuilt, contains a monument to a man who should be remembered. Although he was the bastard grandson of Sir Ralph Egerton whose figure we see in Bunbury church, he was acknowledged and given a university education then became the trusted Chancellor of Elizabeth I. It is from him that the various Egertons in Cheshire are descended. His portrait hangs in the dining room at Tatton Park and he was an ancestor of the Duke of Bridgewater who dug the canal along with those at Oulton Park.

DUDDON

There is little more than the Headless Woman pub to attract visitors although the old hall is now a farm. It is said that in the Civil War a serving maid refused to disclose where the Hockenhulls' treasure was hidden and was beheaded by the Roundheads. In front of the pub once stood a huge ship's figurehead with her head sawn off and fastened to her hand to suit the story. There is uncertainty if the figure was stolen, sold or given away by a landlord who had no sense of history. No one knows where she is now or even if she still exists - the wooden figure that is!

DUNHAM MASSEY

The splendid Georgian hall is now in the care of the National Trust, but its park contains less well known things worth seeking out. The oldest is the motte of a Norman castle, for this was the original home of the Masseys who feature so much in Cheshire history. There were many branches of the family and an old saying tells of: 'More Masseys than asses, Leghs than fleas and Davenports than dogs' tails.'

There is a fine 17th century water mill in a pleasing setting in the deer park, which still has its herd of deer wandering freely and there is a deer house where they are fed and sheltered in the worst of winter weather. Perhaps most poignant are the tombs of the dogs, where favourite companions were laid to rest from 1702 to 1736. The grounds contain a statue of a black man, but despite the idea that it might represent a faithful servant or have some picturesque origin the real story is not half so romantic. During the 18th and 19th centuries there was a fashion for black servants, sometimes slaves, who were dressed in the best, exotic looking costumes and often had their portrait painted with their master or mistress. There was also a fashion for model figures of servants, often holding trays for visiting cards to be left. This statue falls into this category; technically known as a 'blackamoor', it was simply a figure for decorative purposes but intended to look exotic.

DUTTON

Its old hall is well hidden from the readers of this book, for you will have to go to Sussex to see it now, renamed Dutton Homestall. Old timber-framed buildings were always assembled on the ground by the carpenters who numbered every joint. Look at any old timber-framed building and you will see the number codes. So when the whisky distiller Lord Dewar offered to provide a new farmhouse and remove the old one it was not so difficult a task. The Duttons were one of the leading families in the district; their graves have been traced in the excavations of Norton Priory and their arms are amongst those carved in Great Budworth church. However, at the dissolution of Norton Priory many items were removed and taken to build Dutton Hall. The Duttons were responsible for the minstrels of Cheshire (see Great Budworth) and it was at this house that John Bruen enjoyed dancing and 'hunting with great mouthed dogs' before he turned Puritan (see Tarvin). By the 19th century it had ceased to be a 'stately home' and had become a run down farmhouse.

Dutton has other oddities too. After the First World War the whole village was purchased and divided up into equal sized portions which were allocated to ex-servicemen to use to make a living from the soil. Only a little round structure with a metal roof opposite the village pub gives you a clue that the best known feature is invisible underground. It is the Preston Brook Tunnel, the last phase of the Trent and Mersey Canal going to join the Duke of Bridgewater's canal. A second mode of transport left a far more visible reminder: the Dutton Viaduct of 1837 carries the London to Glasgow railway line over the Weaver valley on lofty arches designed jointly by George Stephenson and Joseph Lock, who later designed the first houses in Crewe.

 ## Eastham

Eastham is where the locks open from the Mersey into the Ship Canal, which takes vessels 35 miles to Salford Docks - it never actually reached Manchester! Shipping is now usually too big to use the canal, hence the oil refineries gather round this end of the estuary. There was a time when people driving through the county would stop and stare at a huge ship apparently floating casually through the meadows or at the end of terraced streets. Eastham church has a few Norman stones, an old cross cut down and used as a sundial and ancient yew trees. You can also find graves of young men of the early days of aviation who were killed while learning to fly at the nearby Hooton aerodrome, which was used during both World Wars and the hangars remain. They are not a thing of beauty, but there is a charitable trust which plans to see them preserved as a monument to early flying containing a museum collection.

The Eastham Ferry Hotel was built for the visitors who crossed the Mersey for a day out before the Ship Canal was built. It still does a good trade, but the customers come by car from the landward side for a drink and a wonderful view into Liverpool. At one time it had fairground attractions, exotic gardens and even a small zoo and vied with New Brighton for the Liverpool day trip trade.

 ## Eaton by Tarporley

There are three Eatons, but this one is on a sandstone outcrop in the forest. The old blacksmith's is in the centre of a little triangle in the middle, with quarries close by which were later used for the back walls of houses. Look for where floor joists went into the rock. The cross was one of several destroyed by the Puritan John Bruen with a new cross put on top of the old steps to mark the Queen's Silver Jubilee in 1977. Beyond a farmyard is what has been claimed as the most northerly Roman villa in the Empire. It has been excavated but there is only access by arrangement with the Grosvenor Museum. It has two hypocausts (heating systems) and no doubt felt the benefit so far north! The British Museum of Natural History has a piece of stone unearthed in Eaton quarries in 1812 on which two dinosaur footprints can clearly be seen. Others of the same shape are known (see Bebington) but the Eaton version are three times the size of any found elsewhere, earning the beast the special name *Chierotherum Herculis*. Is it the only hamlet with its own dinosaur?

❧ ECCLESTON

The name indicates that it was a place where an early church was established, from the Welsh word for church. It is at the entrance to Eaton Hall's park, and was a delightful creation by a man with fabulous wealth and a man with a wonderful eye for detail. The Grosvenor money came from a lucky marriage in 1677 to Mary Davis, the twelve year old daughter of a lawyer who had acquired much land around London at the time of the plague and fire. By the 19th century this land had become the most fashionable part of Victorian London and the Duke of Westminster was the richest man in the land. The architect, John Douglas, was one of the best working in the style of 'English Vernacular Revival'; building houses which were traditional in style but up to date in all their facilities and set off by trees and gardens. He did much work in Cheshire, but at Eccleston he created one of the most pleasing and ideal villages in England which has been little altered.

Only the church is not his, but for this the Duke chose G.F. Bodley, one of the Ecclesiologists who studied old churches and tried to build modern versions of them using the best Victorian technology, creating an excellent Victorian Gothic 'high church' atmosphere now much admired. It has the effigy of Grosvenor himself - every inch a Duke in his robes. It rather shatters the image to realise that the title, Duke of Westminster, was given by Gladstone in return for vast contributions to Liberal Party funds and not for great acts of valour.

The entrance to Eaton Park is through the magnificent 'golden gates'. Beyond the park, at another entrance, is a tiny hamlet called Belgrave. It is little more than a lodge and a few cottages and you could drive past without noticing. It was after this that the London Square and the luxurious area called Belgravia were named.

ENGLESEA BROOK

In this out of the way corner of south Cheshire is a little chapel, the Sunday school of which contains a museum of Primitive Methodism. In the chapel yard is a monument marking the grave of one of the founders of the movement, Hugh Bourne (see Mow Cop). The chapel is interesting as it shows what tiny country chapels were like in Victorian times. There were thousands like this all over England which have either been totally altered into dwellings or have seen their little rural congregations fall to such numbers that they can no longer stay open. The museum has relics of the 'Prims' from all over the country including 'preaching plans'. These show how a minister was supported in his work by various local preachers. The minister managed to work his way around a 'circuit' of chapels in a district covering a large area and providing services close at hand for poor people unable to travel far. There are also relics which reflect their worship such as banners carried in processions to attract people to services and loving cups used at 'love suppers' where they were passed from hand to hand, but as they were Methodists the cups only held pure water. Opening times are limited, so check before visiting.

FARNDON

Farndon looks across the 14th century sandstone bridge over the River Dee to Holt, where the Romans made pottery for Chester. Holt Castle was the first place of jurisdiction outside the Palatine of Chester and it was there that the Vicar of Over and the men who killed the Abbot of Vale Royal to prevent him abducting Mary Hector, went to take refuge in 1437. The bridge is said to be haunted by the ghosts of the heirs of Prince Madoc, of Powys, who left the last Welsh princes in the care of the Norman Earl Warren, who disposed of them and the threat of them raising a rebellion by dropping them over the sides in the 13th century. Despite the tale the bridge was not built until 1345!

The street leading down to the bridge is attractive with timbered buildings but the lover of the curious will wish to visit the church, which was almost rebuilt after damage in the Civil War and is therefore one of very few churches built under Cromwell. Its treasure is a stained glass window showing soldiers and arms of the Civil War correct in every detail. Not much stained glass was made at the time for churches, indeed the Puritans were more likely to smash any showing saints. There is nothing else quite like this memorial window to be seen anywhere.

FARNWORTH

In the parish in which Widnes was to develop, the old church contains many monuments to the Bold family and the only royal grave in Cheshire. Mary Patten Bold married Prince Eustace Saphiech of Derekzyn in the tiny principality of Lithuania at Bold Hall, but died just a year later in 1824. The monument was made in Rome and is a superb example of Neo-classical art. She is shown on a Grecian couch, her head collapsed by her husband's heart as he stands over her, both in classical robes. An angel holds an hour glass with her time run out in front, pointing her finger towards heaven, and to one side is a lamp which, symbolic of her life, has been extinguished. There is no sign of grief, their expressions are intended to show a stoic acceptance of fate. The Bold family crest is a griffin and legend says their ancestor killed one, long ago.

FRANDLEY

Frandley has associations with George Fox who founded the Society of Friends, better known as Quakers, and once had a tree under which he preached. It was taken down a few years ago when it became too dangerous, someone's idea of saving it by pouring molten lead into the rotted part contributing to its end. Seven oak trees were planted to mark Queen Victoria's Diamond

Jubilee, giving the area the alternative name of Sevenoaks. However, some of them have had to be removed over the years because they were unsafe, so it is a bit of a misnomer. Here an early meeting house was set up in the 17th century. It has stairs to upper galleries, a covered area to shelter horses and a meeting room without a pulpit or communion table. The Quakers did not have ministers or set services, allowing anyone from those who gathered to talk. A later Victorian building took over next to it and the original building is somewhat in need of more love and care than it gets as a store.

 ## Frodsham

On the now well wooded hills above the town were three Iron Age hill forts looking out over the Mersey, and wide views are still to be enjoyed. One of the forts on Helsby Hill, whose cliff viewed from the road from Chester looks like a male profile, is cared for by the National Trust. Frodsham was a venue for Sunday school outings, with a helter skelter; many children came by salt barge down the Weaver.

Its church sits half way up the hill with splendid views of the river and two strange tales to tell. One monument records: 'Peter Banner, carpenter of Frodsham who died of Dropsy October 21 1749 aged 50. In 33 weeks he was tapped 58 times and had 1,032 quarts of water taken from him'. Another is to Francis Gastrell who died in 1772. He was vicar from 1725. In those days vicars often just took the payment for being in charge of a parish but actually lived away from it, paying a curate to take the services. They were often from wealthy backgrounds and becoming a vicar provided a regular income and no real commitment. Gastrell purchased New Place, the magnificent house Shakespeare had built for himself in retirement. For some reason he fell out with the authorities in Stratford. First of all he cut down the mulberry tree that the bard had planted because people were always peeping over his wall to see it. Then he demolished the house, all but the foundations, and moved back to Frodsham. The church contains Norman arcades, and a couple of stones with Saxon carvings telling of a still older church.

The castle was destroyed in the Civil War and a building on the site is now an arts centre. Edward Abbot Wright, a former owner, missed a train because the stable clock was slow and he ordered that it be kept three minutes fast - and it is still religiously checked each day to be sure it is, more than 100 years later!

GAWSWORTH

This is one of Cheshire's favourite showpieces and needs no introduction, but in a quiet wood owned by the National Trust is a grave with two epitaphs. I will not spoil the delights of reading them for yourself. One was written by the occupant before he died, with a tongue in cheek reason for not wanting to be buried in the graveyard. Its first line; 'Here undisturbed and hid from vulgar eyes', ensures it a place in this book. The grave is of 'Lord Flame' or 'Maggoty Johnson', the last jester in England, whose violin is kept at the hall. He was a dancing teacher and musician and pictures of him in jester's motley are ill conceived. The word jester was a name for a household entertainer which had lost its original meaning. Just as plumbers no longer use lead pipes and computers do much more than mathematical problems. 'Maggoty' does not refer to his remains nor is it derogatory. It was a term used in the 18th century for people who wrote songs. The tunes were supposed to wriggle like maggots in your mind. Indeed, a famous portrait of John Wesley's father shows him wearing a hat with wriggling maggots in it as he was also called 'Maggoty'. In Victorian times a more sombre stone was provided, it looks as if it was intended to cover the writer's own version, and may originally have done so before being placed to the side.

Gawsworth Hall and village are far too well known to describe here but between the hall and the church is a feature not everyone notices. It is believed to be one of the last tilting grounds to survive in England. The old vicarage is also of great importance being one of the oldest timber-framed buildings to survive in Cheshire, probably from the 15th century. It still retains the open great hall with the roof beams exposed above where there would have been a central open fire. This remains a private home.

When he came this way in 1900 Fletcher Moss found the church and churchyard locked. The vicar refused to answer the bell and allow him to see the church. I was reminded of Gawsworth when I saw a different passage which told how the gates in a rood screen were made without locks. This was to represent the fact that although the clergy and choir are in a separate part of the church there was no barrier to anyone wishing to meet their God. Indeed in the wedding ceremony the bride and groom take their first walk together from the chancel gates to the communion table after they are pronounced man and wife. However, when I last visited Gawsworth the chancel gates were well and truly locked. All I could do was peep between the gaps to see the famous Fitton effigies, which were otherwise kept from sight and therefore deserve a place in this book. Many visitors who do not know of their existence probably do not even walk up to the screen to peep. It is a sad commentary on modern living that although the age of the motor car has made a visit to Gawsworth possible for almost anyone, those who visit cannot be trusted to behave in a church. I do not know if it was an act of vandalism or only that one was expected that caused the decision to lock the gates, but it is a sad one; especially regarding the symbolism. There was a time when all churches stood open for private prayer or to admire the historic remains. Those days are long past and many church treasures are not mentioned in this book because the church is not open to visitors or because I did not want to draw attention to something which might easily be stolen from one.

The Fitton monuments were a joy to admire, as they showed the changes in fashion of four generations of the family and their children until the family became extinct. I have told the story separately under the entry for Church Minshull. Amongst those who are represented are Mary, the attractive daughter who showed such promise when she went to the court of Elizabeth I but came back pregnant and in disgrace after a spell in the Tower (see also Malpas). There is also a gruesome 'cadaver memorial' to remind you that all life is temporary. Under the richly clothed figure there is another of a skeleton with worms wriggling in the bones.

The Harrington Arms in the village preserves the name of a family who lived at the hall long after the Fittons and is one of the last true farm pubs with cow byres around a farmyard which doubles as the car park. I do not know if the nearby Fool's Nook pub really has anything to do with Maggoty Johnson. However, in a field close to it a Bronze Age burial was excavated in which was uncovered the only Bronze Age beaker found in Cheshire. This might not sound very significant until you are told that beakers are believed to be the first containers for ale to be used in this country and that the beaker people (who completed the building cycle at Stonehenge) are believed to have introduced the first ale into Britain. So people may have made merry in the nook for a very long time - and more than one will have made a fool of himself!

 ## GRAPPENHALL

This is Warrington's hidden gem of a village, still with cobblestones, the stocks, an old pub and a church, all impeccably looked after as one of the district's showplaces. On the church tower is a carving of a cat (or lion) with a distinct grin. It is said that this inspired Lewis Carroll, who was born in nearby Daresbury (see Brimstage and Pott Shrigley entries). The monument to Sir William Boydell in the church was taken and exhibited in Warrington Museum when it was first dug up in the churchyard, as an inappropriate curiosity. It was returned when tastes had changed and people could not get enough of Gothic things. He is shown as a 'crusader' with legs crossed, his hand grasping his sword.

 ## GREAT BUDWORTH

You need to be a detective to look around one of Cheshire's best known villages, and it has been the setting for detective stories. The first performance of *Murder Most Foul* was shown to the villagers and the television adaptation of the game *Cluedo* was filmed here and at Arley Hall. Many go away quite sure they have seen a typical Tudor village, even books claim it is and some guide books talk of thatched cottages - but there is not one. It was all concocted by the Squire, Rowland Egerton Warburton, and his architects - including the great John Douglas - in Victorian times. They went about the estate looking at what could be saved and got rid of what was beyond saving. Then they used the old timbers to knit together a fantasy place, moving timbers from old farms in the country to cottages in the village street. Some old cottages have been enlarged by adding brickwork between the joints at the corners. The former Ring o'Bells pub looks genuine enough with the date 1706 scratched in a beam by the door but look round the back to find it has a Victorian rear. The 'Tudor' chimneys were all put in to make flues for Victorian cooking ranges although it is said no two are identical.

The church is filled with secrets. Look at the carvings near the roof which are associated with tricksters and temptation. It is one of the few churches in the region where you can detect a theme. You will need some instructions in the symbolism of medieval art; so here goes, but be prepared for here are warnings of evil. Above the pulpit are the Dutton arms but a face on the column opposite has been putting his tongue out at the preacher for years! There are multi-faced heads, inspired by images of pre-Christian gods long after the origin was forgotten, converted to symbols of two-faced liars. There is a green man, an ancient fertility symbol with foliage growing from his face, an emblem of sacrifice but a trickster too. There is an owl; this was a symbol of Jews, who hid from the light of Christ like an owl in the darkness. It is near the door, a reminder that the mythical 'Wandering Jew' who turned Christ away from his home on the road to Calvary was allowed to stop at a church door if there was a service. On the same column is Eve, a naked temptress in the Garden of Eden. You can also spot a fox's head with a goose over his shoulder, a symbol of the cunning Satan who comes in the night to take a foolish person's soul, but also of false preachers and tricksters. Two figures were associated in medieval art with brothels. The cock (also with Peter's denial) and the ape, this one playing bagpipes. The bagpipes are male symbols (think about the shape) and apes were kept in brothels (Hogarth depicted one in *The Harlot's Progress*). The Duttons who helped build the church controlled all brothels in Cheshire.

A Dutton ancestor, Hugh Dutton, in June 1216 led a raggle taggle army of noisy musicians and beggars to relieve Earl Randle who was besieged at Ruddlan Castle by the Welsh at the time of Chester fair. The Welsh fled thinking it was the band at the head of a great army. So the Duttons were given authority to licence all musicians in Cheshire after holding auditions each year. As musicians were often employed in brothels he licensed them too - how the brothels were judged is not recorded! So you can detect a double significance of music and brothels in the ape carving. They were not intended for vulgarity or titillation, but the medieval church showed such images as a warning of what **not** to do. Most British examples were removed by Puritans and prudish Victorians. As this group all have double meanings they have survived because their true identity was not recognised.

Hanging on a wall is an old panelled door. A matching fragment is in the County Museum collection, and the two together indicate that it was part of a memorial to John, Vicar of Budworth. This was John Bracegirdle, who went from here to be Vicar of Stratford where he baptised William Shakespeare. He taught local children including John Brownsword, who followed him to Stratford as master of the Grammar School, where he may have taught Shakespeare; he later moved to Macclesfield and has a memorial in the church there. Take a look at the effigy of Sir John Warburton of 1575. One side is richly carved, the other very roughly, which shows that it was made to be in a wall alcove where one side would not show. On the font are carved symbols of the passion, but they are on one side only, showing that when this was put back in place the builder didn't consider them very important. Carvings on the tower include St Christopher and the Virgin, emblems of Norton Priory, and amongst others is, apparently, the boar of Richard III, perhaps giving an idea of the date.

Look at the stocks too. On the right pillar are remnants of hasps to hold the hands, for this was the whipping post. Note also the warning above the George and Dragon:

> As St. George in arm'd array did the fiery dragon slay,
> So might thou, with might no less, slay the dragon
> drunkenness.

It was penned by Warburton, the rhyming squire of Arley, who was responsible for closing two other inns in the village. Perhaps the warning was needed as at the nearby 'Cock o'Buddoth' on the Warrington road, 'Drunken Barnaby' enjoyed the ale so much that he had to be helped to his room by two porters in the 18th century. There used to be pictures of him which reportedly went with the old landlord when the pub changed hands.

GREAT WARFORD

When Charles II was asked to return to the throne he agreed to tolerate the Puritan way of worship, although the Church of England was restored as the state religion. He did not make it easy for them though, insisting that any meetings were held at least five miles from the nearest church, and outside the times of services held there. Effectively, this was either before six in the morning or after six at night. An old barn at Great Warford was converted to a little Baptist chapel in 1712 after these rules were relaxed. It is still very much as it was then with an old pulpit and dark oak box pews in a Puritanly plain interior. The oldest gravestone is dated 1671, long before the Act of Toleration allowed Nonconformists to worship in towns and it is believed that the congregation had been meeting in the old barn before the conversion during the time of restrictions. Early Nonconformist meetings often took place in barns as they could hold a small congregation, out of the elements, until they could afford a proper chapel. Accounts of the people who worshipped and were buried here show that many lived several miles away but were prepared to travel on foot in the dark, to worship as they wanted to.

A row of old cottages has been converted into a large pub and restaurant which was known by the posh name of the Warford Arms. For some reason all and sundry in the neighbourhood knew it by another name which it adopted officially about 50 years ago. If you get a blank look when you ask the way to the Frozen Mop it is because many locals still call it 'T'Frozzun Mup', sounding the 'o' as in frog and the 'z' as in zebra.

HACK GREEN

Some of the strangest signposts in Cheshire point to the 'Secret Bunker'. It is not secret any more, but was in the days known as the Cold War when nuclear war between Western Europe and the USSR seemed likely. At the end of a long lane, under a simple looking store near an old black and white cottage there was an underground base. It was equipped with all the latest technology. Everything was on hand from which to govern this part of Britain after a nuclear catastrophe. Today you can go

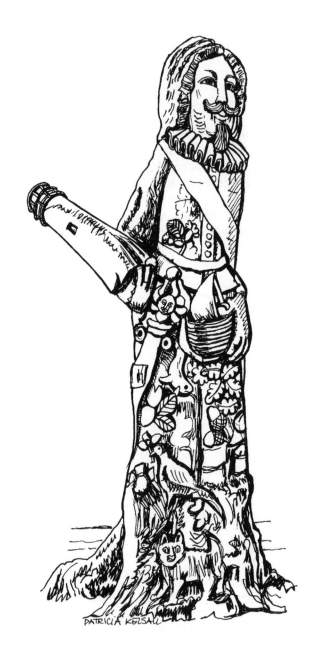

'The Childe of Hale'

to visit one of the strangest attractions on the tourist trail. If it was not for its signs it would remain one of the most hidden secrets of Cheshire.

HALE

This one is on the north shore of the Mersey and not to be confused with Hale and Hale Barns now in Greater Manchester's millionaire belt. It has plenty of visitors with a lighthouse as a landmark. The seeker of the curious, however, looks for a little nature reserve and in the middle will find one of the few surviving duck decoys. Rather than take pot shots at flying birds the canny owner simply set some captive ducks in the centre in cages and left them to make their mating calls. Wild ones were lured to swim along the ever narrowing channels into the cages where they were trapped and killed for the table.

Everyone who visits hears about 'The Childe of Hale', John Middleton who was 9 feet 3 inches tall. According to the *Guinness Book of Records* the tallest men today are comparative shorties at 7 feet 10 inches. He went to London in the hope of finding fortune at the court of King James I in an age when monarchs surrounded themselves with the curious. He upset the king by injuring a favourite with whom he had been told to wrestle, but was given a pension and sent back to Hale where he is buried in the churchyard. His imagined portrait is on the pub sign and a fanciful tribute has been to carve one of the trees which died of Dutch elm disease into a representation as a focal point near what is left of the church. Unfortunately the church was almost destroyed by fire and only the walls and tower remain. His cottage is still standing, though it is doubtful if the windows in the gable end were really put there so that he could sleep with his feet sticking out of them!

HALTON

Much of Runcorn dates from the time it was a 'New Town'. In Roman times there was a defended settlement on the hill. The Castlefields estate which now covers it was the largest council housing estate built under New Town legislation.

The Cheshyre Library

The old castle was started by the Norman Barons of Halton, but some of what we see is actually make believe of the 18th century when it was restored to make a picturesque view from Norton Priory. The Castle Hotel was built to serve as the courthouse for the Duchy of Lancaster, with the sessions room reached by an imposing staircase and the royal arms above. The bar was where prisoners were held - it did not serve drinks then! I once explained to a group of students that the castle had been part of the Duchy of Lancaster and asked if they knew who the Duke of Lancaster is. When I explained that it was the Queen a wit chimed up, 'What night does she serve behind the bar?'

The hill has wide views over Cheshire and the village contains some fine old sandstone buildings while next to the church is the Cheshyre Library. A small building with two large windows, it was given in 1733 to contain books on theology, law and classics for use of local gentlemen and though its books have long since lost their relevance the building remains as a meeting room by the church. It was the first public library in Cheshire, and given during the 'Age of Reason' or, as it is sometimes known, 'The Enlightenment', when people believed that knowledge was all important and that gaining knowledge of every aspect of the world would improve their mastery over it.

 ## HARGREAVE

——— Hargreave's church of 1627 was given by Thomas Moulson, one time Lord Mayor and Alderman of London. The story is that when he was a child he had to go to school in Tarvin. On trying to return one night he and his friend found the River Gowy too flooded to try to cross and spent the night sleeping in a haystack. They both vowed if they became rich enough they would build a church and a school in Hargreave to save anyone else the indignity. It is a long plain structure as originally it was a church and school joined together, with his name and date above the door. The Gowy seldom floods any more as it passes through the oil refineries, the owners having spent considerable time, effort and money on making that as unlikely as possible to keep their site dry.

 ## HARTFORD

——— This is Northwich's 'West End' where the wealthy settled as the wind blew the smoke in the other direction. When the church was built an old lady complained about being forced to sit between a soap boiler and a salt maker. They were Sir Joseph Crosfield and Sir Joseph Verdin but their's was new money from 'trade'. Its railway lines were also an attraction for those building grander houses. Although two cross here their stations are a mile apart as they were operated by rival companies. When the first line was built in 1837 they found Roman burial urns which are now in Warrington Museum. Until direct lines were built to Manchester and Chester, mail for those cities was unloaded here to be taken by fast horse and rider.

As it had a 'First Class Station' long enough for express trains, Lord Stallibrass, a director of the railway company, built his house next to it and the express trains stopped for him. An incognito visitor was the Prince of Wales, later Edward VII, who came to visit his friend the Earl of Enniskillen. The Earl once took the blame when the Prince was summoned to court to answer charges that he had fathered a child by another man's wife. The Prince could keep his activities a secret, walking unrecognised through the streets here. Even today some London trains stop at this village station and it was the only village served by Intercity trains before privatisation, with daily commuters to the city. The pub by the station had large stables so that horses and carriages could be hired to take travellers home to any part of the county. In the yard behind is a mounting block made from the original 1837 stone sleepers on which the track was laid.

HASLINGTON

The half-timbered mansion was built by Admiral Sir Frances Vernon in 1545, despite a local tradition that it was made from wood from the Spanish Armada, which was not launched until 1588. Vernon was given the job of dismantling the ships and doubtless some of the furnishings and fittings from them came back to Haslington and over the years people changed the story so that wooden furnishings became confused with wooden beams. The house, which is now a farm, is a splendid example of its period and is surrounded by its moat. The village also still retains other good timber-framed buildings including the Hawk Inn though the date 1510 is a bit optimistic, the style is of more than a century later. The olde worlde inscriptions carved on the beams are also a bit of imagination, only a few years old.

A sign pointing to the historic Wheelock Heath Baptist Chapel takes you into a lane with what looks just like local authority houses except that the walls are covered in texts about the poor. They were built to replace the chapel almshouses and the inscriptions were reused.

HAVANA

The first mill was founded in this village in 1761, and shortly after the British took Havana during a war with the Spanish, so the mill and village were named after the victory.

Slowly trade changed, but its name proved a temporary salvation. It was quite legal and honest to label things made there as 'made in Havana' and an industry making cigars from imported tobacco leaves was set up. This avoided the heavier tax on ready rolled cigars. In 1902 an American import law demanded that the name of the country was put on all products and customers only wanted cigars that were made in Cuba. People moved away in search of work and it was known as 'Cheshire's deserted village'. Today the motor car allows people to live more than walking distance from their workplace and the row of workers' cottages have been restored. To get to them you go down an unadopted road and cross a bridge over the Dane with an impressive weir which once powered the mill, but you must turn round and come back the same way. Not far from the turning, in Eaton village, is the Plough, an old pub looking over a green with an even older secret behind. A timber-framed barn was rescued from decay in Wales and is now the restaurant.

HERONBRIDGE

Just south of Chester by the River Dee various Roman structures have been found, perhaps a centre for Celts who relied on the fortress for business. Under Roman buildings, skeletons were found of the victims of some long forgotten battle. You can still make out the remains of an earth bank. It is conjectured it may have been involved in the fighting between the pagan King Aethelfrith of Northumbria and the Christian Britons between AD 605 and 607. Before one battle the King saw some men standing to the side. When he asked who they were he was told they were monks from Bangor Isecoed further down the Dee, who had come to pray for his defeat. He ordered they all be killed before the battle started for if they were against him with their prayers they were as much against him as if they had held swords. The account of the battle says 1,000 monks died that day, but this is probably an exaggeration to make the deed sound more bloodthirsty.

High Legh

Modern housing from Manchester's commuter belt has taken over what used to be the parks of the Legh family homes. There are old stocks which look quite out of place by a pavement in an otherwise ordinary suburban street and an old private chapel with a memory of an event which in a quiet way changed history. In 1813 a young lad came here to work as a garden boy, and it was here, many years later, that he said God had revealed his plans for him. He was Robert Moffat who became involved in the growing Methodist ranks, becoming a minister and then setting off to work in South Africa. He could have made a reasonable living preaching to the converted in the prosperous settlements. But instead he moved more and more into the north. The Boers there believed that the natives had been created to be their servants and used them as slaves. Moffat tried to change their opinion. He went further north, preaching to those who had never heard of Christianity, nor seen a white man. He wrote down all he saw and did, hoping others would follow him and sent the texts back to be published in England. It was a book by Moffat that influenced David Livingstone to become a missionary in Africa and he married Moffat's daughter.

Hill Cliffe

South of the Mersey and well away from Warrington, an early group of Nonconformists started to meet here after the return of Charles II when they were not allowed to meet in the towns. A local farmer gave them a piece of land for burials in 1643 and the first funeral took place in 1664. Local historians in the past were not always so keen on accuracy as in telling a good story, and here the tradition grew up that Oliver Cromwell had not only worshipped in the church but actually read the lesson. It was a tempting idea as he was known to have been in Warrington and his statue was, and still is, near the bridge. As the earliest gravestone was from after he died, a couple of forged ones were slipped into the chapel yard to make people believe the story. Of course in his time there were no dissenting chapels, for Cromwell and his followers took over the Church of England and the parish churches. However, there are still those who would rather believe a good tale than the boring facts of history.

HOCKENHULL

Hockenhull Platts, just south of Tarvin, is an old name for a bridge. The main road from Nantwich to Chester crossed the Gowy here where the stream runs in several shallow channels. Often it is hardly enough to wet more than the soles of your shoes but it can flood after heavy rain. In the Middle Ages three little bridges were built for pack-horses to cross in the wettest of weather. The road diverted onto a better route for wheeled traffic long ago and you must park and walk up a well marked footpath known as Baker Way to reach them. An application made for help from the magistrates in the 17th century stressed that the poor local parishioners could not afford to pay for repairs, pointing out that people who used them came from as far away as Wales and Yorkshire. They are not exactly as pack-horse bridges would appear; they did not have side walls so that the packs could cross undamaged, but walls were added long ago for safety.

HUXLEY

Huxley's old hall, surrounded by a moat fed by the River Gowy, with a bridge and scrolled pediment above its gateway, is only part of what was once a much larger house, and is now a private residence. Professor Huxley was descended from the local family. It was he who defended Charles Darwin in the great debate about the theory of evolution at Oxford when he was asked if it was on his father's or his mother's side that he was related to an ape. He decided to find out more about his family history (but not quite as far back as the apes). As a scientist he was not to know that often the only time people were mentioned in medieval documents was when they appeared in court. He found the Huxleys had been there several times in disputes with the Abbot of Chester and constable of Halton and decided it was, perhaps, best not to enquire further.

On a quaint corner is the disused Hoofield blacksmith's forge. You can see his anvil, a wide iron ring in the ground which was

Hockenhull's three medieval bridges

used when fitting metal tyres to wooden wheels and an iron cone used to shape barrel hoops. Most amazing is a huge tower of horseshoes all welded together. Just how many horses contributed their footwear is not known, but it is certainly a sight to seek out. Near to it at Brook House the road makes a sharp bend around some pools which were specially created for black swans in a little nature reserve.

HYDE

Hyde was a product of the cotton industry but is now virtually a solid continuation between Manchester and Stockport. It has memories of poverty as well as prosperity, including that of John Prince, 'The Bard of Hyde', a poet whose memorial was put in St John's church long after he died and who was buried in a pauper's grave.

In the churchyard can be found a little stone epitaph with its own tragic tale. Fanny Bush was one of a party of Kalahari bushmen. They were in a travelling show which came to Hyde in the days long before television documentaries made us aware of the realities of Africa and conservationists gave us different attitudes. Then, shooting animals to stuff and put in a museum, keeping them alive in tiny squalid cages to be stared and laughed at and even bringing native people in a sort of human zoo were accepted as ways of entertaining and educating people. Bushmen, because they were tiny and wore hardly any clothes, were particularly interesting. Fanny caught tuberculosis, a one-time incurable disease which often came from drinking milk in the days before pasteurisation or even germs were understood, and died here.

INCE

Cheshire folk said 'Go to Ince' to imply 'get lost'. The name is Celtic for island and although today the Mersey marshland has long been drained it is still in a way an island on a little hill and surrounded by industry. There are still marshes frequented by wading birds beyond the Ship Canal, which you can see from the churchyard. To reach Ince you travel through a science fiction landscape of oil works until deep within you come upon this hidden gem. An old tradition tells how the fairies moved the church from Stanny to this island - was it to save it from the future oil works? The area developed as Britain's oil refinery as the tankers became too big to use the Ship Canal, but the deep anchorage, flat land and good communications here made an ideal spot for development both for the industry and for housing the people who work there.

The impressive ruin of Ince Grange, a massively built sandstone manor house belonging to the Abbot of Chester, is currently being investigated by archaeologists. Turn left at the village square and it can be seen towering above the road. A warning notice advises you not to enter. Close to it are the restored stocks, while on the other side of the road outside a modern row of bungalows is an old iron water pump. The stone to rest the bucket on has a groove on two sides showing it was once the weight in an 18th century cheese press. The remnants of Stanlow Abbey have long vanished behind the works and there is no visible indication that an abbey once stood here before flooding and a fire caused the monks to move to a drier place at Whalley in Lancashire in 1279. Also lost behind the works is a curiosity. In order to get the water from the River Gowy into the Mersey it is siphoned in pipes to go under the Ship Canal.

 ## KELSALL

On a clear day they say you can see Blackpool Tower, but I must admit I never have. It does have an amazingly wide view of the western part of the Cheshire plain. Particularly the oil waste burning above the works of the Mersey: especially exciting after dark when it looks like a beacon flaming over some pagan altar - or does my imagination run too wild? I always wish the authorities would place an observation lay-by there so I could stop for a while, but presumably road safety won't allow that. You can take the old road through the village with several pubs and an old stone lock up, threateningly placed outside the Royal Oak to hold drunks overnight.

People have enjoyed local produce for over 2,000 years as the Celtic field systems around the Iron Age fort at Kelsborrow Castle prove and Kelsall has a tradition for fruit production. In the past going to Kelsall to pick fruit was as much a part of local culture as going to pick hops in Kent was for Londoners. Since the advent of the motor car people often pay to pick their own soft fruit. As European regulations have made it illegal to sell traditional Cheshire apples an enterprising grower now sells them as juice and cider. A local folk song chorus proposes the toast:

> Here's to Cheshire, here's to cheese,
> Here's to the pear and the apple trees
> And here's to the lovely strawberries.

KNUTSFORD

Two houses close to each other overlooking The Heath are associated with the famous. The Cam House is said to have been the home of the local highwayman, although the present house was built after his time and used the old name. Edward Higgins was a skilled criminal who first appeared in court as a sheep stealer in Worcester in 1727 and was acquitted. In 1754 he was transported to Maryland for house breaking in Worcester. He used the money to live in style in Knutsford when he returned, attending the hunt or balls as a gentleman to see who had the best jewels. He put woollen socks on his horse to ride out at night so that there would be no noise to attract attention and helped himself. When things in Knutsford became too hot he moved to French Hay in Carmarthenshire, where he was eventually captured by the constable in Laugharne. He had tried to open a chest with one of his own keys which had broken in the lock; the remaining part matched a stump on his key ring when he was arrested. He was hanged at Pensarn, a part of Carmarthen where executions were carried out, on 7th November 1767. That was only part of the story - now see Sale for the rest!

In the other house Elizabeth Gaskell, the novelist who immortalised the old town as Cranford, lived. She was born in London but sent to live with her aunts in this quiet place of 'elegant economies' when her mother died. Her simple grave is in the Unitarian chapel in Brook Street; a plain structure erected sometime after 1689 when Nonconformists were first allowed to have chapels in towns and where her husband was minister. She was a friend of Dickens and the Brontes, who wrote important works which drew public attention to the poverty of industrial Manchester. There are Cranford memories all over the town including the tower set up to her memory by Richard Harding Watt. Behind are columns from the old church of St Peter in Manchester outside which the Peterloo Massacre took place.

Watt built the Ruskin Rooms in Drury Lane, as a meeting place for discussions and lectures on mind improving topics. They were financed by a laundry in an adjacent building with a chimney to resemble a mosque minaret. The laundry closed in an age of washing machines and the chimney was demolished as unsafe. The whole is now offices.

Watt was a glove maker turned architect and produced fantasy buildings in Italian style. In Legh Road is what Pevsner described as 'the witches' coven' of decorative Italian-looking villas. They have little ledges or holes for birds to perch and Mediterranean details including pantile roofs. When the film *Empire of the Sun* was made the director Stephen Spielberg could not find anywhere in Singapore that looked like old Singapore. So Legh Road was pressed into service with the addition of bamboo fences! Sir Henry Royce used to sleep in a tent in the garden of one of the houses where the Rolls-Royce partnership had been officially agreed and which is still marked by their emblem. Opinions differ over why he did so, between that he felt it was healthy or he had fallen out with his family!

An interesting aspect of the old railway station is the way it was designed for sexual segregation in days before equality was an issue. The platform going into Manchester had no waiting room as it was for businessmen and others who would arrive for their regular train into town punctually - and in those days trains could be relied upon to be punctual too! The other platform was often used by families who were heading for holidays in Wales. On either side of a large clock was the general waiting room, and the ladies' waiting room where ladies and their maids could wait without the need of a chaperone. They had fireplaces and seats for people who might arrive early with all their baggage for their holidays, or who might come from Manchester and send a porter to order a carriage home.

Dominating the town is the courthouse designed to look like a stately home but without windows by the great classical architect Harrison, from money raised by the River Weaver Trustees (see Runcorn). It had an interesting period when, no longer used for criminals, the cells were used as a 'Test School' for men who had served in the First World War and wanted to enter the Church. It was organised by 'Tubby' Clayton who founded the group Toc H. The lectern he used in the prison chapel is now in the parish church and is made from the metal of shell cases collected on Flanders fields, a parody on turning swords into plough shares.

One interesting feature of Knutsford is the narrow pavements; many date from the end of the 18th century when Lady Stanley, a sister of the Earl of Derby, gave the money for them. She insisted they were only one stone wide to prevent couples walking arm in arm which she disapproved of. When she died she left money 'for flags in Knutsford' but when the authorities wanted to decorate the town in honour of Queen Victoria they interpreted the term broadly and instead of spending the money on flagstones purchased banners instead.

Overlooking Knutsford is the huge red brick church at Cross Town. What is claimed to be the base of the cross is now kept in the porch having been used for a time as a font. The outside looks genuine enough, square below and octagonal above with good medieval heads on the corners. However, where there should be a square socket for the cross there is a round bowl. The Victorians were not above changing things to suit their needs so there is no reason why it should not have been changed to a more suitable round socket.

Directly in front of imposing Booths Hall is a stone monument, wrongly termed 'the obelisk'. It looks as if it might have once been one of a pair of gate-posts. By tradition one of Knutsford's two ancient chapels stood close by and tradition says it is made from the stone; you can still see the foundations set out as a feature. The other chapel is recalled by the sign on the White Bear pub showing the bear in a pulpit. A joker took a bear into the chapel and into the pulpit where he put his paw on the Bible. The Bishop closed the desecrated building for a year and charged the town for the cost of reconsecrating it.

It is fitting that Knutsford May Day, one of the oldest festivals of its kind (it was revived in 1864 when interest in all things medieval was at its height), should have a little mention here, for much that makes it special and unique is not always obvious. The parade has always included children from the town's schools, and even the workhouse in the early days, and some of the traditional costumes are antiques in themselves. Many favourites such as the old woman's shoe, complete with her children, Grace Darling in her boat, the village wedding, Robin Hood and his Merry Men, Higgins the Highwayman and the Cranford Lady in her sedan chair have paraded for over 100 years. Jack in the Green, the walking bush, is a relic of the green man fertility symbols which in turn derive from the 'wicker images' of the Druids. He can claim a free drink at any pub as in days of old, but no doubt he needs one or two on a hot day! Classical writers tell us of the Druids who made human sacrifices by burning them in 'wicker images of their gods', and of course the Celtic peoples worshipped gods in the form of trees - something we still remember when we 'touch wood'.

No motor vehicles or advertisements are allowed in the parade, only carts pulled by magnificent horses with shiny brasses and ribbons in their manes. The May Queen's landaus are traditionally loaned by the Lord Mayor of Liverpool. The custom of sanding, making pictures and mottoes from coloured sands, is said to go back to when King Canute crossed the Lilly Brook and scattered sand from his shoes in front of a bridal couple, wishing them as many children as there were grains of sand. Family planning was not a consideration then! Every year a new crown is made and is given to the Queen to keep. Shops exhibit crowns and dresses many years old in their windows on May Day. For the bands and dancing troupes it is the first event of the season, the chance to show off new uniforms and routines. The Heath where the fair is held still belongs to the people of Knutsford though it is now looked after by the Council, and it features in Elizabeth Gaskell's *Cranford*. The whole country's attention was fixed on it more recently as the setting for what was called the 'Battle of Knutsford Heath' confrontation between the two candidates in the 1998 election!

LANGLEY

It was this small valley near Macclesfield which dressed the fashionable world of the Victorian period. In 1826 William Smith opened his mills which were powered by water. The little valley became lined with works and chimneys of the largest hand block silk printing, dying and finishing works in the world, and the stream sometimes ran in amazing colours. It used a variety of processes including the use of waxes to prevent the dye colouring parts of the pattern. It was best known for block printing using over 90,000 different wooden blocks to make up patterns by laboriously using one after another - but never all the lot at once! Later silk screen printing - what else should you do on silk? - was introduced. They even perfected the art of printing onto knitted artificial silk which was cleverly marketed as 'art silk' in the 1930s. A little community developed where the skilled workers lived close to their employment.

Fashions changed and with the growing availability of low cost man-made fibres the market for real silk dropped as prices rocketed after the Second World War. The intensity of labour needed to print each piece of fabric added to the already high cost of real silk which became more expensive to import. Meanwhile people used to cheap machine-made goods and plastics complained if a block was slightly out of position and about the tiny spots which allowed each block to be lined up with the next. These signs of good quality and expert craftsmanship were taken as signs of second rate goods in an age of mass production by people who should have known better. Fashion had yet to discover the 'ethnic' look and handcrafted goods reminded them of home-made things. Markets slowly dwindled and in the 1960s the works closed. Its precious blocks, each one a craftsman-made piece with delicate carving or cast brass-work to print the pattern, were dispersed as curios and ornaments.

 LEFTWICH

The part of the district of Northwich south of the River Dane is known as Leftwich and was in the parish of Davenham. It contains some interesting features, for example the buildings in part of London Road are all raised and reached by steps. This is because this area was likely to flood and the steps are to keep the floors dry. The last big flood was in 1946, after which the odd Bridge House was raised on steps so that its floor was above the high water level. To stand by it and realise that the water was so deep is remarkable enough. That is not the only story. It once stood by the side of the River Dane, but continual sinking flooded the cellar and then the bar, so that customers had to move upstairs. There was substantial refurbishment and the barrels actually hung above the bar in 1909. Then the whole pub was put onto the sort of rollers they used to launch boats in the shipyard on the other side of the road and moved to a safer place. The launching of boats on the Weaver was remarkable in itself for they had to go in sideways as they were longer than the river is wide. There were several shipyards in Leftwich and at one of them Lawrence of Arabia supervised the building of a spy vessel with radio links which was successfully used in the Second World War. Now England's only floating hotel is close to the boatsheds.

Leftwich has other curios, including the Drill Field which is claimed to be the oldest football pitch in continual use. Next to it a timber-framed church, built to replace one which was destroyed by salt subsidence, has been converted into a chemist's shop. Timber buildings of this sort, with reinforced plank walls built in the same way as floors are normally made, were common in the salt towns. They are exactly the same as those which existed in the west of America at the time though no one knows which one copied the other.

The story of the timber-framed buildings is only one of those told in the unique Salt Museum which is housed in the former workhouse and explains this ancient industry. Amongst the curios are a pair of clogs and a boat made from cotton and matches, both of which have been covered in sparkling salt crystals. Hidden away, but available for serious students to study are the finds from the Roman site on Castle Hill, including a fine Roman helmet. The Technical Schools which were built to mark the Diamond Jubilee of Queen Victoria in 1897 now serve as a gallery for temporary exhibitions, but are also worth seeing for some magnificent Victorian stained glass.

LINDOW

At Lindow Moss near Wilmslow the preserved Lindow Man was found in 1984 and is now in the British Museum (see also Shotwick). Do not confuse the Common with the Moss, for the Common is an area of open ground given to the town to mark Queen Victoria's Diamond Jubilee in 1897. The Moss is a mass of peat, the name deriving from the Celtic for 'black lake'. Remains of at least three bodies were found in commercial peat cuttings for agricultural use, including the famous one which the press named 'Pete Marsh'. He was killed after first being given a meal which included burnt bread, and he had mistletoe pollen in his lungs, perhaps he had worn it as some sort of head-dress and had died in the winter-time when it flowers. He had been hit on the head then garrotted by a leather band, then his throat was cut before he was lowered into the peat as a sacrificial offering. The date at which he died is not certain as the Carbon 14 dates for the body are a couple of centuries older than that for the peat in which he was buried, which was not laid down until AD 100. When the skull of Lindow Woman was found in 1983 it prompted one local man to confess to the police that he had buried his wife on the Moss 20 years before - it was not his wife but he still faced trial for murder! Similar 'bog people' have been found throughout Northern Europe and it is believed that after being feted for a time in the middle of winter they were ceremonially killed and offered to the water goddess as sacrifices.

LITTLE BUDWORTH

The little church has a curious feature in a font made of fossil limestone. In it can be seen countless pieces of crinoids - or sea lilies. The word crinoline comes from the Latin word for a lily and the bowl is fluted like a large shell. In it are sections of the stems of the crinoids that compose the stone and you can see slices through the tubes. It is quite philosophical to think that the babies of Budworth are baptised in a font which is made of stone created in a tropical sea millions of years ago. Memorials in the south chapel include one to Sir Philip Grey Egerton to whom the commander of the fort at Balaclava in the Crimea surrendered his sword at the battle in 1854. A stone which can no longer be identified in the north side of the churchyard was to Henry Lovett, who was buried in 1745 at the age of 85. He was the 'King of the Gypsies', who met regularly on the heath in bygone days. The north side of any churchyard was used for suicides, criminals, vagrants and any others outside the normal parishioners.

LITTLE MORETON HALL

It is probably one of the most photographed buildings in England, so the hall itself is not the subject here, but two little round mounds, one inside and one outside the moat. They are not big enough to be the places where the earth was piled when digging the moat, and usually this was spread onto the island to help raise the dry part. Instead they probably had summer houses on the top. The Elizabethans loved intricate gardens with flowers and shrubs laid out in designs which were like expensive fabric. The best way to admire them was from above, and little structures or arbours of trees were provided for people to sit and meditate, sheltered from the sun.

The hall itself is an example of what has been called the 'unit plan' of architecture where each wing is separate. This is not only because they were built at different times, but so that they could be used independently. The guest bedrooms and long gallery above the entrance would be used when visitors came to stay, so that they could live separately and the family could get on with their own business. It seems strange to modern ideas but the great architect Paladio is known to have designed his villas in just this way, and even Georgian mansions had smaller family rooms for use in the winter when the grand entertaining rooms were put under dust sheets.

It now proudly displays one of its old 'garderobes', a simple toilet from the seat of which was a long drop into the water of the moat. When it was excavated they found broken chamber pots which are on show along with numerous shoes. A pot dropped down one is understandable but the shoes are part of an ancient fertility ritual. The Museum of Leather in Northampton carried out considerable research into what was once a widespread custom. Often a single shoe is found hidden in a recess or in the roof. Somehow they were believed to bring good luck and children to a home. Little Moreton now has these secret talismans proudly on show.

 ## LOWER PEOVER

We turn down a little opening from the road between Knutsford and Middlewich, into a corner that time seems to have

The memorial to Warren de Tabley, poet and naturalist, in Lower Peover churchyard

forgotten. Only the children playing in the village school remind us that it has not stood still. There is also a little school, still with its bell turret of 1710, now converted to a house. The picturesque outside of the church is actually a Victorian restoration, but there are old timber columns and beams inside which date from the 13th century when the villagers were allowed to have their own chapel because travelling to Great Budworth was too far. It still has its Jacobean box pews with the coats of arms of the various families who rented them painted on the door and at the back are shelves on which the charity bread was placed - to be collected after the poor had sat through the service.

The south chapel has much of interest. There is an old chest carved from a solid piece of wood - chests like this gave us the word 'trunk' as they were cut from a tree trunk. In days gone by a Cheshire wench had to show her worth by lifting the heavy lid with one hand, to prove she could cope with butter and cheese making. On the wall is a carved wooden hand, no one is really sure what its origin is, but it may represent the hand of St Oswald, a famous medieval relic, as it did not decay when he died. There is also a large monument to Geoffrey Shakerley of Hulme Hall, who distinguished himself during the Civil War battle of Rowton Moor. When messages needed taking to the King in Chester he rowed himself over the Dee in a washing tub, with his horse at his side, to bring them from the Welsh side away from the Roundhead ranks.

It was this chapel which caused a long law suit between the Bolde Lady, Mary Cholmondeley (see Malpas), and her cousins the Shakerleys from Hulme Hall, over who had the right to sit in the chapel and to go out of church first in the processions after the services. Until not so long ago the church had no vestry and the choir would march out from the door under the tower and in through the front door of the Bells of Peover pub which acted as the vestry. I always imagine the good Bolde Lady marching at the head of the parade to get the best place in the bar! The name is derived from the family of Bell, who owned the pub for many years, not from the church bells.

In the churchyard there is an extremely tall cross to the memory of Warren de Tabley, a poet and naturalist of Tabley Hall. He studied blackberry briers and established a famous brier garden at Tabley. One species was named after him and still grows on his grave as a living monument. The churchyard wall does not seem to have caused any writer to comment on it before, but I do not know of another wall like it in Cheshire. In fact the only other walls I have seen like this are at the deserted village of Wycoller in Lancashire where they are said to be ancient walls for cattle enclosures. It is made of large slabs of stone, like paving stones set on edge. It would be an unlikely way of using stone even in a stone rich area but I would think each of these must have been carried for at least ten miles. It is illustrated as early as 1815.

 ## LOWER WITHINGTON

St Peter's church is a rare treasure, a splendid 'tin mission' perfectly preserved. Stone churches are commonplace in Cheshire, even the old timber-framed ones are well looked after, but most of the tin missions have long ago decayed and gone to the scrap heap. It was, perhaps, wartime use of the material which gave corrugated iron a bad name for in late Victorian times it was a new and exciting building material. Much was produced in Ellesmere Port for the Wolverhampton Company. Places which could not afford a masonry church could buy a tin mission by mail order, which arrived like a construction kit to be put together and used until there were funds for something better. Often they were built in expanding towns or in poor country areas. Lower Withington's survives intact and should be recognised as the treasure that it really is. The area is now affluent and it would be a shame to see it replaced by something like the smart village hall on the other side of the road, which caters for more modern tastes and needs.

 ## LYMM

The road here crosses a little valley on a dam rather than a bridge, created in 1824, which has made a very attractive lake a central feature. Near it is a slitting mill in which iron sheets were cut by water-powered machines to make wires and nails. Its remains have been excavated and preserved for us to see. Crosfield Bridge is a reminder of a scandal which nearly put an end to ICI before it was even formed. Brunner Mond of

Winnington agreed to supply William Lever of Port Sunlight with soda ash for his soap at favourable rates. However, for some reason the Co-op got better rates and Lever threatened to open his own soda ash works using local brine supplies at Lymm. He purchased land and planned a second Port Sunlight. However, the company agreed to pay damages and avoid legal action. Lever used his money from this case for several purposes in Liverpool including the first Department of Town Planning at the University and purchasing the old Bluecoat School as an education and arts centre. In 1926 Rosco Brunner, who had been most severely implicated in the scandal, shot his wife and then himself rather than face disgrace.

Several rows of houses in Lymm still have external staircases leading to long lofts on the third storey. These were where fustian was cut. In the old days it was made by weaving special grooved wires into cotton cloth to make something which resembled coarse velvet. Afterwards a special knife was put in the groove and each loop opened up when cut to make a piled fabric sometimes known as 'moleskin' which was much used for workers' clothing in Victorian and later times. Mellors (*Lady Chatterley's Lover*) wore fustian trousers. I wonder if they were made from fabric from Lymm?

The church is Victorian and replaced one with a story. An old woman would collect rain water in buckets from the drainpipe on the church roof because it got clothes much cleaner than well water. She was told this was disrespectful but continued until one night a skeleton hand came down the pipe, grabbed her bucket and after hitting her on the head with it went back up taking the bucket. At one time Lymm and Warburton had the same vicar and an old Cheshire threat was to 'tear you Lymm from Warburton'. The men in grey suits did just that in 1974 as Lymm is still in Cheshire while Warburton went to Greater Manchester.

MACCLESFIELD

It is an old town capped by the church of St Michael. David Simpson was the parson of St Michael's, but after he preached against Sir William Meredith of Henbury there was an outcry amongst the local gentry so the Bishop of Chester removed him from office within a year of being appointed. Charles Roe built Christ Church for Simpson to continue to preach in Macclesfield and it was completed in just seven months so that the first service was held on Christmas Day 1775. Simpson was a powerful figure who often raised the huge Bible in one hand as he stood towering above the terrified congregation in the tall pulpit. He was not averse to throwing the cushion on which it rested at a member of the congregation whom he saw asleep and he even ordered them to stay in their places when an earthquake rocked the church on 14th September 1777. John Wesley speaks fondly of the church in his journals and preached often from the pulpit. Early Methodist ministers are buried in its chapel yard where several of them lie in what is called 'The Vault of the Seven Methodist Saints'. Roe was determined that his church should have a higher tower than St Michael's, which had the advantage of being on a hill, and so the tower looks strangely out of proportion. He was the first to bring silk mills to Macclesfield, and also worked the local copper mines, making his own Macclesfield halfpennies when there was a shortage of small change. His monument is in his church and he is one of the founders of the Industrial Revolution. However, when his daughter died she left her sedan chair to St Michael's where it stood for many years before being sent to Styal Museum for conservation. It was to be used to bring old or sick parishioners to church. If you get to the church by climbing the 108 steps up to it you may start to appreciate how useful a gift the chair would have been in such a hilly town. If you decide to climb the hill stop off at the Castle, one of many 'real ale' pubs in the town, but this one has splendid Georgian plaster ceilings, and the cellar is said to be part of the dungeons of the old castle - though I have my doubts whether the big key on show behind the bar was actually the one which locked the castle door.

Inside St Michael's are many monuments with fine effigies especially to the Savage family, including that Sir John who helped Henry VII to victory at Bosworth. A strange memorial brass attracts those who seek curiosities. It shows Roger Legh with his six sons kneeling in prayer before a picture of St Gregory receiving a vision of Christ to show that the Communion bread really was his body. An old woman had mocked the bread saying that she herself had baked it and how could it be holy. Under it is an inscription which records that Legh was pardoned for 26,000 years and 26 days: a unique survival of when pardons were sold. It was this practice that so upset Luther that it sparked the Reformation and Chaucer included a pardoner in the Canterbury Pilgrims. Outside the chapel an unthinking workman has cut a section out of an equally interesting gravestone for a drain. It records how Mary Bromfield saved £5 out of a pension of ninepence a week to pay for her funeral in 1788. There was an early friendly society which helped widows to do this in Macclesfield at the time.

The little museum was given by Miss Brocklehurst who was with the writer Amelia Edwards for part of her voyage of *1,000 miles down the Nile* which became a Victorian bestseller. It includes her collection of Egyptian relics and has barely changed from the day it opened in 1897. However, the duck-billed platypus, one of very few in the country in 1897 (when science was not sure if they really existed) has mysteriously disappeared from the side of the giant panda since I first visited. Children in this conservationist age can hardly believe the tale that Captain Brocklehurst went to Asia especially to shoot a panda and have it stuffed for the museum. The item which proves most amusing in an age of sexual equality is the iron brank. Iron branks were a form of punishment for nagging women in 17th century Cheshire and are sometimes known as the scold's bridle. An iron cage fitted around the head with a lock at the back and a metal section to go into the mouth to prevent the tongue wagging. There was often a chain at the front by which the unfortunate woman was tied to a post in the market or in the house. Chester, Congleton and Stockport still preserve their branks and the Stockport one in the Heritage Centre is particularly vicious with large metal spikes to go inside the mouth. Chester appears to have been a centre for making them and an old couplet is recorded:

> *Chester presents **** with a bridle*
> *To curb women's tongues who talk too idle.*

In the park look out for a huge boulder carried here in the Ice Age and the remnants of stone crosses. They are not like those seen at Sandbach for they have round shafts and are a type which came when the Norse pushed this way from Northumbria.

MACCLESFIELD FOREST

There were never many trees here as a 'forest' in this sense was a place for hunting. The Davenports were the Royal Foresters and had the right to execute felons - for each one they received a salmon from the Dee so there was always a good supply. Their crest was a felon's head with a rope around it, you will find it on several pubs in this area and in their old homes at Bramall Hall and Capesthorne.

The Forest has its own 18th century chapel for people who lived high on the moors. Its setting is in rolling moorland, and a splendid drive or ramble to find it repays the effort. It is surrounded by grouse moors; many of the former vicars were keen falconers, one of them took his birds into church and perched them on the communion rails for the service. Another wrote under the name of 'Peregrine' for *The Field* magazine. In such a remote place 'evensong' was actually held in the afternoon so that people could see to walk home safely at all times of the year. The church registers record the burial of several people who were lost on the moors in bad weather and starved to death. The annual rushbearing could attract hundreds of people in Victorian times who walked from Macclesfield and surrounding areas so that there were too many to fit in the church and the service took place in the churchyard, surrounded by the moors and the calls of the grouse.

MALPAS

Malpas was a centre of baronial rule in Norman times and the mound of the castle is next to the church, which is a well known and attractive building with a sad and little known tale inside. On the tomb of Randle Brereton and his wife are carvings of their children. One of them became involved in intrigue as he was a favourite at the court of Henry VIII who gave him the stewardship of Longdendale. Then Henry decided he no longer wanted to be married to Anne Boleyn and Brereton was beheaded on an invented charge of adultery with her. On the end of another magnificent tomb of Elizabethan times in the Cholmondeley Chapel, the couple's son Hugh is shown in prayer with his wife Mary. He was the first MP that Cheshire sent to

Westminster, for until his time the County Palatine held its own Parliaments in Chester. Mary married into the family bringing her own estates of Holford and was one of the most forceful personalities of her age. She purchased Vale Royal Mansion and entertained King James I there in 1617. He wanted to have her sons at court but she refused saying she was too proud to take a favour. The King called her 'The Bolde Ladie of Cheshire'. Perhaps she remembered the fate of William Brereton and her cousin, the unfortunate Mary Fitton of Gawsworth, who was a lady in waiting until she was sent to the Tower by Elizabeth I when she became pregnant. Mary Fitton is believed to be the 'dark Lady' who was the inspiration for Shakespeare's sonnets.

The east window is in memory of the once famous son of a rector here. Bishop Heber of Calcutta wrote hymns including *From Greenland's Icy Mountains* and *Holy, Holy, Holy*. The local school is named after him.

It is said King James I spent the evening with the rector and his curate when he visited Malpas and that the rector treated his curate so contemptibly and then refused to buy the King his drink, that James declared they should both be rectors and equal. Sadly for romantics, the double rectory goes back much further and may derive from the fact that parts of the parish were in Wales - nor indeed would King James have gone anywhere 'incognito'. The large three-legged chair in which the King supposedly sat is preserved in the Red Lion Inn. I took a friend to see the King's chair recently but was told it was kept in the private part of the pub, upstairs, in case of damage - so it is yet another item which is actually hidden and can no longer be seen. However, the framed set of illustrations to 'Diana Woods Wedding' are still on the walls. They are by Ranulph Caldecott, who came from an old family living in the hamlet of that name just to the north of Malpas. He started work in a bank in Victorian Whitchurch, but his unique style of line drawings filled in with colour wash was ideal for book illustrations. His drawings were often used in nurseries and schools to illustrate children's poetry, besides appearing on Christmas cards during the first half of the 20th century. Local houses and churches can sometimes be recognised in the background to his pictures.

Marbury (northwich)

Probably more nonsense has been written about this place than anywhere else in Cheshire! The Smith Barry family (who also used the Irish title of Barrymore) built it and in its latest phase it resembled a small Fontainebleau. Before the Second World War it had become a country club with its own swimming lido. Then it was used by a succession of military occupants during the war, before the former barracks were used to house Polish refugees. Now Marbury is administered by the County as a Country Park, preserving its Victorian landscape features after the old hall was demolished as beyond repair.

Two interesting survivals are a hollow believed to have been used for cockfighting and the ice house facing the mere. During winter blocks of ice were cut from the pure waters and stored here in an underground chamber shaded by trees. The first ice house in England was built for Charles II who had seen them on the Continent. He sent his gardener (aptly called Mr Rose) to Fontainebleau to study them and amazed his guests by serving strawberries and ice cream. They were never used for storing food, nor was the ice put in drinks (a 20th century invention) but blocks of ice were placed into compartments of specially designed metal-lined cabinets completely separate from the food compartment and used to cool iced desserts.

Marbury has associations with Bluecap (see Sandiway) and the horse 'Marbury Dunn' who won a bet of 500 guineas by running from London in the round of a clock and died when it drank icy water straight afterwards which stopped its heart. It is said to be buried in a linen shroud with silver shoes on its hooves. Some local pubs take their names from Marbury horses including the 'Spinner and Bergamot' and the 'Drum and Monkey'. An even more unlikely legend is of an Egyptian lover of the heir to the house who came to live here but would not attend church. The cold climate proved too much and before she died she begged to be buried at Marbury. When a future heir sent her to a grave at Great Budworth the haunting started and she was returned to Marbury. A second attempt was to throw her into Budworth Mere, but she floated back to shore in a lead coffin! At last she was buried under the rose beds at Marbury in 1938. When the local press investigated the story in the 1960s old folks who had worked at the hall said the body was actually an ancient

Egyptian mummy. That is quite likely for many country houses had an Egyptian collection in an age when it was fashionable to visit Egypt and 'return with a crocodile under one arm and a mummy under the other'! It once contained one of the finest collections of classical sculpture in any private home in Britain.

This must be the only place where the police have been sent to investigate a ghost and actually took it back to the police station! About 20 years ago frightened motorists phoned the police to say that they had seen the 'Marbury Lady' on a dangerous corner. Officers went out to investigate and found an old polystyrene head which had once been used to display hats or a wig in a shop window, with some net curtains swaying at the end of a fishing line which had been put there by jokers.

 ## MARBURY CUM QUOISLEY

This was said to be the prettiest village in Cheshire, but a development of local authority housing can hardly be counted as pretty. Its old church overlooks an attractive mere, hence the name which translates as 'fortified place by a mere'. You do not see the water until you have driven up a narrow lane to the churchyard and walked round to the other side. Near it seats have been provided and you can watch the bird life. Outside the Swan Hotel there is a huge oak tree, planted to mark the victory at Waterloo. Its visitors often come this way by boat along the Birmingham branch of the Shropshire Union Canal which enters the county through the locks at Quoisley.

Although the place is delightful, it is the roads and lanes through which we drive to get there that are the significance of this area. They are in undulating land unlike that in other parts of the county. For these hills are evidence of the last phase of the last Ice Age. In a final thrust the ice came down, around 10,000 years ago, leaving much of Cheshire as if it had been ironed flat. The ice sheet only came this far, and the hills are part of what geologists call the Ellesmere Terminal Moraine. That is, material left at the edge of the ice. On a sunny day, especially when they hold their annual 'Marbury Merry Day' it is difficult to imagine that it is on nothing more than debris piled up by the ice.

MARPLE

Samuel Oldknow opened a large cotton mill here in 1785 and used children from the workhouses to do much of the work. Fire destroyed the mill but there is a churchyard, with a tower without a church and a church without a tower! Oldknow built the first church in 1808 and his monument along with others including one showing a teacher with his class are preserved in the tower. The church proved too small for the expanding town so it was taken down and replaced by a bigger one in 1878-80, but funds ran out before it could have a tower built. So they simply utilised the old one for the bells. Another pioneer of industry had a part to play, the engineer who designed the canal aqueduct was Benjamin Outram who set up the Butterley Company in Derbyshire. He was the first man to manufacture iron rail lines and it is said that the term 'tram' comes from his name. By the locks near the aqueduct there is a splendid warehouse which served Oldknow's mills and the spectacle of boats passing through the locks or over the aqueduct is still colourful.

MARSTON

The Lion Salt works here are the last of the old type, which used huge open pans as big as swimming pools to boil brine pumped from under the ground. It is hoped that one day they will work again, but there are exhibits in the old Lion pub that became the works office. They are by the canal side, on the other side the road runs through the centre of a circular lake on a causeway. This is the remains of the Adelaide Mine which was the last salt mine in the area. At one time mines were a venue for special events as well as mining; as when two Russian Archdukes visited one to see it illuminated with hundreds of candles and to eat from tables tastefully set out with flowers.

When, like all the others, Adelaide flooded and collapsed in 1928 the 'Flash' soon filled with water to become a haven for wild fowl including great crested grebe. Nearby Ashtons and Neuman's Flashes also mark where mines collapsed, but they have been filled by waste from the nearby works of ICI. They have a special almost surrealist botanical secret. They are the home of rare lime-loving orchids. The original seeds 'hitched a lift' on the wheels of rail wagons bringing limestone from Derbyshire to be mixed with brine for the production of soda ash in the works. They found a foothold and flourished in the lime here.

MARTON

There are two, one a village with a magnificent half-timbered church and an ancient oak far too well known for further mention. The Whitegate Way footpath passes through the other rural hamlet, following the route of a former railway line which once served the salt works of Winsford. Near to where it passes over a railway bridge is the stone base of a 14th century cross which the abbey ledger says was set up by order of Edward I to mark the abbey boundary. It is broken and now resembles a large armchair known as the Wishing Seat - try it for yourself. On the other side of the former railway, and visible from the embankment, is the moat of Marton Grange, a former farm of Vale Royal Abbey. It is on private land so do not go further than the Whitegate Way. The moat still retains the abutments of a drawbridge, although the splendid half-timbered house was demolished in the 1840s. Between the moat and the old railway track are two hollows, believed to be fish pools in which the fish were allowed to lay, before being forced back into the moat. When they were big enough to survive the young fish were allowed to go into the moat to fatten, eventually to be caught and provide food for the abbey.

The local pub is the Plough, recalling an ancient legend and tradition. The Devil, after whom the Boggart Brook is named, tempted Friar Francis with offers of three wishes. He agreed on condition that he could keep what he wished for even if the Devil failed to provide the final part of the bargain. He asked for food and drink for the rest of his life and a dozen hay bands (ropes to bind the harvest) made from Marton Sands. The Devil could not make even one and from then on the locals ploughed the sands in an annual festival to make sure he never did. Until the 1960s the Plough only had a six day licence as Lady Delamere who closed the pub in Whitegate village was offended by people going there for a drink after service on Sunday. If you are out for a drive amuse your friends by taking a diversion to Nova Scotia;

a little group of cottages and a farm which was settled by a Scottish family in the 19th century.

🌿 MEADOW BANK

──── This area of Winsford gets a separate mention because at the end of a long road you will find the only working salt mine in mainland Britain. You can't go down except with special permission, but it is worth making a detour in autumn to see the huge stockpiles of salt that build up each year in time to melt winter snow and frost on our roads. It forms a natural shell called 'thatch' and can be stored outside.

The Weaver here was navigable for sea-going vessels, though none come this way any more, and the wide locks are worth a look. It was perfecting these locks up to the former salt works that ensured Leader-Williams was given the job of designing the Manchester Ship Canal. He also drew up plans to continue the Weaver as a ship canal through Stoke to Birmingham! The old railway line which took coal to the salt works and salt to markets has been closed down to become the Whitegate Way country walk. Look at the banks and in places you will see that they are supported by something that looks like stone sponges. This is 'bass', a sort of slag left after burning poor quality coal. In Victorian times houses in the area were actually built of bass. It must be the only place where workers lived in houses made of the waste from their industry.

Despite this the river gave us a legacy of great beauty, for in the mid 19th century it was the way that the ships bringing china clay came to the Potteries. The raw Cornish clay was taken from Winsford by pack-horses. Without this Wedgwood and the other great 18th century potters could not have made their advances in producing china. He intended originally to bring the Trent and Mersey Canal to Winsford Wharf but problems with subsidence in Northwich made him change his plans. A word of warning; don't set out to visit after winter snows or ice when lorries from all over the country queue to restock.

MELLOR

You will find stories of buildings which have been moved in various ways elsewhere in this book, but Mellor was a whole village which changed its address no less than four times! Well, actually it stayed just where it had always been, but they changed the boundaries around it. Until 1936 it was happily in Derbyshire, and it has much in common with that county but it was given to Cheshire as it was easier to provide essential services. In effect it is one long street of millstone grit houses climbing the hill away from Marple and it was easier to bring in water, gas, electricity and the post this way. In 1974 it was given to the former county of Greater Manchester, and now finds itself in the Metropolitan Borough of Stockport but still keeps its Cheshire postmark! There is not much that is 'metropolitan' in this village on a hill set in fields with dry stone walls. You turn off the main street into a country lane at the end of which there is the church and vicarage and the starting point for scenic walks.

The site has been shown by archaeologists to have been occupied in the Iron Age and Roman periods. The church was rebuilt in the 19th century but has two older curios. One is a huge Norman font, the other a wooden pulpit, which makes claim to being 'the oldest wooden pulpit in Christendom'. The churchyard has the remains of the old stocks and whipping post. While most curious is the stone of Joab Brierley. He was infirm and deformed and had a stone coffin specially made to measure during his life into which he, and only he, could fit. It attracted so much attention as it lay in the churchyard waiting for his death that the vicar ordered it to be buried until it was needed. The eccentric man was a member of an exceptionally secretive branch of the Freemasons. So he arranged for a gravestone to be carved during his lifetime with masonic symbols and inscriptions which were so complicated that although he left a space for his 'egress' (exit) to be included on the stone no one ever completed it. Perhaps there was no one who understood enough to know where to put the date?

Meols

A vanished village which once existed near the Hoyle Lake, we do not know much of Meols' story from the history books although enough survived to be included on John Speed's 17th century map of Cheshire. At high tides remnants are sometimes washed up. Some come from its submerged remains and others from ships which were wrecked along the coast. Wirral folk were well known for plundering, and even causing wrecks. Prehistoric, Roman and medieval objects have been found, many of which have made their way to museums in Chester and Liverpool.

The sort of things which have been found here are puzzling, for most are made of metal. While it is possible that all the pottery was broken up and destroyed by the sea or that the old time collectors only looked for metal and ignored pottery, it does not really explain why so many of the items are precious objects such as coins, brooches and other jewellery, knives and weapons. There is another possibility. We all know the story of King Arthur who sent Excalibur back to the Lady of the Lake. This is believed to be a folk memory of offerings to the water spirits in Celtic times. Many precious objects have been dredged from the bottom of rivers, especially the Thames, where they were given as offerings to the river goddess. Not far away, when building work on the Valley Airfield on Anglesey was taking place during the Second World War a great number of Celtic objects were found in a former bog there. Were at least some of the objects from Meols offered to the waters in this way, perhaps here, or perhaps in the great estuaries where the action of the tides eventually delivered them to the beach here? It might be significant that the majority of the objects date from the time before Christianity which would have discouraged such offerings. In this context it is worth remembering how Lindow Man was offered to the waters.

Not far away are the Hilbre Islands, with reserves for nesting birds and seals which can be reached at low tide, but take great care as the tide can change quickly. There was a church maintained by Chester Abbey, and also a pub and salt works were recorded in days gone by. A cave is known as the Maiden's Grotto, and recalls the tale of a girl who was being sent to North Wales, or Ireland (depending on the version of the tale), to an arranged marriage against her will. Unaware that the man she loved was following to rescue her, she threw herself overboard in an attempt to end it all before marrying without love. She was washed up on Hilbre, and found a temporary shelter in the cave where she told her story to one of the monks before she died.

MIDDLEWICH

Middlewich was the Roman town of Salinae, making salt and other things which were sent up the Roman road known as King Street to soldiers in the North and later those who guarded Hadrian's Wall. Pottery dates suggest it was set out as a main supply road - a Roman M6 - to take supplies to Carlisle for distribution, around AD 80-90. You can see finds from the site in the town library including items associated with salt making. It was the Romans who first developed salt making in a way which was to remain largely unchanged until the 17th century. They exploited the rich lead deposits of North Wales almost as soon as they invaded this part of Britain. Lead ingots (pigs) have been found near Chester marked with dates around AD 70. They were keen to get at the lead as they had the skill to extract silver for coins from it. Spare lead was probably brought by water to mid Cheshire to be made into rectangular 'pans' around a yard wide in which the brine was boiled to make salt. This was needed by the invading troops to pay each soldier his salt pay from which we get our term salary. Experts believe the Romans first arrived in the industrial settlement of Salinae (the salt works) soon afterwards. Lead salt pans with Roman names have been found in Northwich, Middlewich and Nantwich. Most of the Roman settlement has been built over but finds show that for over half a mile, both sides of King Street must have been lined by timber buildings acting as workshops and homes. Where the River Dane is joined by the Croco there is a Roman fort which has been traced by air photography. This may have served both as a posting stage along the road and as a police base from which to supervise the industrial settlement. Because it is so well preserved it was decided not to touch the fort and it has a football pitch set out on it. Another fort has been traced where the canal makes a sharp bend south of the town. The Croco would have been a much more important river in Roman times but James Brindley diverted the water into the canal and left it as nothing more than an overflow channel so it can claim to be Cheshire's hidden river.

The Big Lock pub on the other side of the canal from the Roman fort is a reminder of an abandoned plan to join the Trent and Mersey Canal to the River Weaver at Winsford with a wide section along which sailing barges could come to the salt works direct from Liverpool. When the plan was changed it went through tunnels only wide enough for narrow-boats instead and not for wide sailing barges to reach Runcorn. The town is a Mecca for canal people, particularly in summer when the whole place bursts into colourful song for the annual Folk and Boat Festival. Two canals meet here, built by the two great canal engineers: James Brindley constructed the Trent and Mersey which is here joined by a branch from the Shropshire Union complex by Thomas Telford. That was built so that boats from the Midlands could avoid the congested tunnels and locks in Runcorn and go to Ellesmere Port. The Duke of Bridgewater did not want to lose the tolls from the locks and insisted there was 100 yards of land between the two. They were only joined in 1835 - after he was dead! By the junction is a pretty lock-keeper's house with a hatch in one of the windows where the tolls were collected. The Cheshire Cheese pub reminds us that special fast 'fly boats' took cheeses to Liverpool for the London market as they were considered the finest in the world 'not excepting the Dutch'. Middlewich made special dairy salt which helped give the unique taste.

By the church porch is a gravestone to Anne Barker, with the inscription:

> Some have children, some have none,
> But here lies the mother of 21.

In the south chapel, now a vestry, is a tiny brass picture of an Elizabethan Lady Venables with her three children kneeling in the fashions of her day. The Venables were Barons of the Cheshire Parliament which was held at Chester when the county was ruled as a Palatine under the Earls. Their home was at Kinderton, just outside the town where there is still a moated enclosure and a little mound, next to a road junction. It is one of the least impressive monuments to be seen in the county. It is too small for the motte of a castle but may have been for a summer house from which to observe the elaborate gardens, as with similar mounds at Little Moreton Hall. Archaeological survey has discovered the remnants of such gardens in the fields. One of the Venables killed the Moston Dragon, which you can find carved in wood in the church (see Moston). The estate then passed to the Venables family. When the last Venables heiress died in 1715, the estates passed to the Vernons of Sudbury in Derbyshire, whose crest of a boar's head gave its name to a pub nearby.

MOBBERLEY

This is England's largest parish and, despite nearby Manchester Airport's second runway, it is still quiet with old inns and country lanes. Its church has many delights including the stocks by the churchyard wall and a splendid Tudor rood screen. The woodwork was carved around 1500 and contains coats of arms of local families, but it is a little picture in a stained glass window which brings the curious. It shows Everest with two tiny figures climbing to the top. They were George Leigh Mallory, son of the rector here and Andrew Irvine, son of the historian from Birkenhead, who were lost to sight on the mountain in 1924. In May 1999 came news that the frozen body of Mallory had been found very near the top and was buried there. There was no clue on the body about what happened, though his name was still embroidered on his shirt label. He appeared to have fallen to his death and no sign of Irvine or the camera which they took with them was found. No one knows if they reached the top but they certainly went higher than any other climbers had reached at that date. The rectory where he was born was given to the National Trust for safekeeping. It is still a home and not open for visitors, but like the window it will keep the memory of Mallory alive.

A less known, but lovely, tale is depicted in the window next to Mallory's, where we see a representation of a little known poem by Kipling. Eddi the priest had prepared for a midnight mass on Christmas Eve but no one turned up at the lonely church of St Wilfred. Then slowly the door opened and in came an ox and an ass who had been attracted by the light. He remembered that first Christmas night in a stable far away and in the candlelight:

> 'How shall I tell which is greatest, How shall I tell which
>   is least?
> That is my Father's business', said Eddi, St Wilfred's
>   priest.

In an out of the way single track lane appropriately signposted 'Graveyard Road' is a small walled enclosure surrounding the Quaker graveyard. Quakers refused to be buried on consecrated ground; this field belonged to one of the community who met at nearby Morley and put a corner aside for them. When tales of ghosts were investigated some years ago it was found that the slime trails of snails on the walls had been reflected by a car's headlights! The local Quakers resented paying tithes to Wilmslow church and one of them took his tenth hive of bees to the vicarage as demanded. When the door opened he removed the straw skeff leaving the honeycomb and bees to the vicar who was entitled to the contents but not the hive!

In an attractive corner the Roebuck Inn is a reminder of the proverb that 'you can tell a Mobberley man by his breeches', which were made from buckskin after a night poaching in one of the nearby parks. Another tale tells of the poacher's wife who was gently rocking a cradle while the bailiff searched the house. Sleeping soundly in it was a young buck which was soon to provide their meal! Today there is a colourful bird garden next to the pub with many bright exotic species to admire.

 ## MOSTON

There is a stretch of water here and when I cross it I always stop and ask anyone who is with me what they think it is. Some say a canal, others a river, then I ask what we are on and they realise it is a solid bank. In fact the river that formed it ran over rock salt many feet below, slowly dissolving it as the brine was pumped out in the salt works some distance away. It is in fact a flash - an old word for flooded land.

You can also drive down Dragon's Lane if you turn off the road between Middlewich and Sandbach, but you will not find the dragon that once lived there. It was killed while devouring a baby by one of the Venables of Kinderton Hall near Middlewich, and:

> A dying dragon bathed in gore
> Which e'en in death an infant tore
> In arms he thenceforth proudly bore
> Emblazoned on his shield.

In fact it was the crest on the helmet - but that wouldn't scan! You can see a carving of the dragon on the 17th century carved screens under Middlewich church tower. He was a wyvern, a type of dragon with two legs and two wings. The modern street sign still says Dragon's Lane on the road between Sandbach and Middlewich.

MOTTRAM IN LONGDENDALE

In the extreme east of old Cheshire, one of its best features can never be seen, but you can feel Captain Whittle's wind all right. It is said to have carried his coffin away when they brought it to this old hilltop church in the 17th century. Inside is an effigy, its feet resting on what is said to be a faithful dog. It is not old enough to be the crusader Ralph Stone, known as 'Old Roe' who was in prison in the Holy Land and had a dream that his wife was about to marry. Then he awoke by the road near Mottram just in time to stop the marriage. No one recognised him except his dog as he was in prison rags. The story is repeated in various versions in other places, for example at Wigan, but it seems to have more to do with the story of Odysseus who returned from Troy in time to stop Penelope marrying than actual events. Roe's Cross can still be seen supposedly marking where the dog met him. This monument in fact records Ralph Staveley and his wife who lived at Staveley Hall which gave its name to Stalybridge.

No church in Cheshire has a more lofty position, with many steps leading up from the millstone grit houses below, and a blue plaque in memory of Edmund Shaa who gave money to the church (see also Woodhead). From the top of the steps the view is like a fortress and the name War Hill suggests it once was. Practically all the stones in the churchyard are flat because of the winds. One tells its own tale:

Though once beneath the ground his corpse was laid,
For use of surgeons it was thence conveyed
Vain was the scheme to hide the impious theft
The body taken, shroud and coffin left,
To wretches who pursue this barbarous trade
Your carcasses in turn may be conveyed
Like his to some unfeeling surgeon's room
Nor can they justly meet a better doom.

There was no law against taking bodies, but had the shroud or coffin been taken then a charge of theft was possible.

The old Court House has an elaborate Victorian drinking fountain set up to record when piped water was laid on in 1888. After listing the officials the mason has added 'for drinking on the premises'. Was this wit, or a warning to those who might carry buckets away to avoid paying water rates? Perhaps the cast iron spikes on the trough were to protect it from metal buckets. Next to it the stocks look as if they are waiting for convicts from the court, but were actually moved here when an estate was built near Hattersley, and next to them is the strangest item, which looks just like a flag-pole. It once had a crown on the top, hence the name 'Crown Pole', and was set up to commemorate the coronation of George III in 1760, perhaps to serve as a maypole.

On Stalybridge Road is a fairly ordinary looking house with a plaque to commemorate L.S. Lowry, the painter who captured the look of the industrial North West better than any other, and who spent his retirement there. He died in 1976 having recorded a vanished way of life. Although Salford lays claim to him with a new art gallery and centre bearing his name he moved to this part of old Cheshire, and many of his paintings contain images of Stockport viaduct in the background. The Manchester Art Gallery acquired the contents of his home, and for a time one room was exhibited in the gallery just as the artist had left it. At the time of writing it is not certain if the contents of the room will be put back into that gallery which is closed for improvements or will go to the new Lowry Centre. However, this artist whose works are the epitome of old Lancashire must be listed amongst the famous people who have made Cheshire their home.

Mottram St Andrew

Known for its magnificent 18th century Hall, now one of the grandest hotels in the region. In the 18th century it was a great livestock market, but that moved to the station at Chelford when the railway was built. The stump of an old stone cross by the roadside was the centre of the market where more than one wife was said to have been sold. It was not so uncommon as one would think in days when the only record was in a church register and many people did not bother with wedding ceremonies, especially if they travelled about the country. Women had few rights and doubtless some women were willing to be sold like cattle to get rid of a bad husband! Other places in Cheshire have tales of wife selling, including Stockport and Macclesfield, where a married man purchased two on the same day in 1799, one for 2s 6d, the other for just a shilling (5 pence!). What his legal wife said is not recorded.

Moulton

Moulton was once a very insular village with one road leading in and the other end leading out. It was the product of the 19th century when cottages were built for the salt workers, along with a church, school and shops making a totally self contained community which was known as 'Little Hell' to outsiders in the depression years when most of the salt works closed down and there was no work.

The village, however, was known for its crow dance. Unusually this was performed by all male dancers, most of them dressed as crows, who danced around a scarecrow which had homing pigeons stuffed into its clothes and at various times they would fly out. After a complex ritual of steps forming different positions the farmer would emerge and shoot a crow. All ended happily with the scarecrow, resurrected crow, farmer and all dancing out together. Just what the origins are is not certain. It certainly has much in common with ancient rituals, but villagers told of it being devised by an old dancing teacher in the 1920s. In those days it was billed as 'The Relic of the Cornfields' so perhaps he simply formalised some older dance. It was performed during the depression years at local carnivals, and if the dancers won first prize a special homing pigeon was released so their friends could join them for a drink in the pub. If no bird arrived there was no money for a drink. I understand that in later years the drink element became more important until the womenfolk stopped their men from taking part. A simpler version is still performed from time to time by the village schoolchildren.

 ## Mow Cop

Standing high on a hill overlooking Cheshire, the 'castle' is only a folly built as a summer picnic shelter for Rode Hall and to improve the view in 1754. It is an early example of the use of Gothic style (most follies at that time were imitations of classical temples) and sits astride the Staffordshire border.

As Methodism spread into the United States there were vast areas of prairies which had farms miles apart and no place of worship. They held 'camp meetings' where the families would come together on a Sunday travelling by wagon, bringing food to cook over camp fires and to worship together in the open air. The Methodist authorities were happy about this in America but did not want to encourage it in England as there were plenty of chapels. They were afraid of spreading diseases and that immoral behaviour might occur if so many young people came together. This was defied by a group from the Potteries who held their own version of the Sermon on the Mount on Mow Cop, where preaching was from farm carts. The movement grew and formed a separate branch from the main church. They called themselves Primitives as the idea was to regain the enthusiasm of the early church holding services in the streets, parading with banners and giving a much more lively aspect to worship. The chapel now houses a museum of Methodist relics.

In an old quarry is a large standing stone left by the workmen, which does not seem to have any purpose. It is called 'The Old Man of Mow', but I understand that this has nothing to do with an elderly gentleman but indicates a phallic shape - 'the old man' being a Cheshire euphemism.

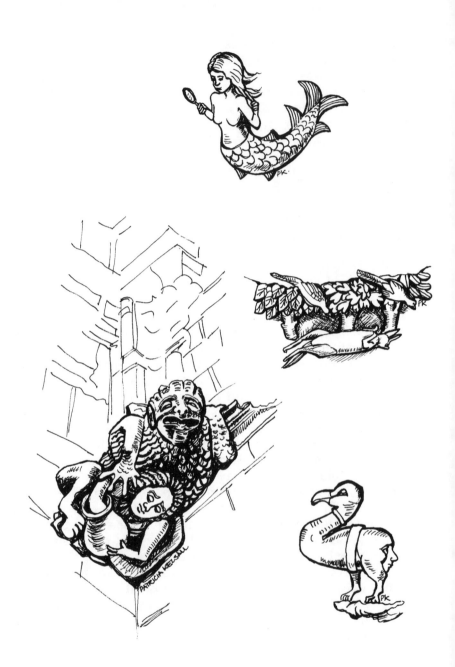

Carvings from Nantwich church

NANTWICH

The huge church, known as 'the cathedral of south Cheshire', was built as a chapel of ease as the salt town grew up in Acton parish. It has been suggested that the builders fled when the Black Death struck the town, leaving it for a century or so before it was completed. Evidence for this is that a vaulted roof was planned for the north chapel but never built, and that the clerestory windows above the aisle are from more than a generation later than the rest. It was being built at the same time as Vale Royal Abbey and masons working on this church would have known, and possibly worked on, the abbey. There are several doors with 'Caernarvon Arches' in which the stones at the top project to support the lintel giving a shouldered shape. They were invented by Walter of Hereford, who was moved from Vale Royal to finish Caernarvon by Edward I - did he design these arches to support soft Cheshire sandstone?

It is said that the wood for the choirstalls came from Vale Royal, perhaps the carvers did too as they are amongst the best in England. The seats lift up like cinema seats but under each is a little ledge on which to rest during long services while looking as if standing. Each is carved with its own scene, a hidden picture book of medieval life. There is a fight between husband and wife while the pig runs off with a chicken on a spit and a dog has his head in a cooking pot at the sides, wrestlers, a mermaid, and the story of Reynard the fox who plays dead so that when birds come to investigate he will catch one. On either side are foxes dressed as friars, as the medieval church loved to show false preachers this way. There are many fighting wyverns (two-legged dragons) which are said to be a pun on the dialect way of saying the river name Weaver. In one the Devil is seen holding the mouth of a woman open - was she a gossip? There is the story of the unicorn, which can only be captured if a virgin sits in a wood, when it will place its horn on her lap - a story which probably resulted in woodland frolics in the past! The best is a strange bird wearing a hood, if you look at the back it is actually the face of someone, the tail being obviously the parson's nose. They are not, as was once believed, simply for the craftsman to have a bit of fun, but each one has a moral, for example the fighting animals represent the conflict of good and evil while the mermaid is vanity with a mirror.

The south transept contains an alabaster effigy of a knight of the time of the Black Prince with its legs carved away. In the past shepherds are known to have done this to get at the alabaster which was powdered as a cure for sick sheep. There is a splendid monument to John Smith and his wife, who are actually buried in Wybunbury where their monument stood for three and a half centuries, but when that church had to be demolished it was rebuilt here for safety. As an heiress she has her own coat of arms; women have theirs on a diamond-shaped 'lozenge' so the tomb has both a conventional shield and a lozenge on the front. The chapel has another secret; the chairs were made in the 'mouse man's workshop' in Yorkshire and if you look carefully you will find the tiny mice carved on the wood as signatures.

Outside in a corner facing the market is another carving of the Devil with a woman, but this time she has her hand in a pot. It is said an old woman took a daily collection from the masons to pay for their midday meals. When they realised that she was helping herself she lost her job but gained immortality in this way as they took their public revenge.

The museum in the former library has exhibits about the Cheshire cheese industry as well as the story of the town, but there is a less obvious museum too. The front of Welch's is only wide enough for a shop window and a door with the Victorian tiles declaring it to be a Pork Butcher's. Inside it is no wider, but stretches back far beyond what one would expect. In old towns it was impossible to build sideways so shops extended to the back, this one has taken over the rear of a neighbour's with a cafe which contains a reconstruction of a shop with products, packaging and fittings in a museum showing shopping before supermarkets.

The town maintains a monument to an American air pilot who realised his plane would crash. Rather than escape himself he steered it away from habitation, but died in the attempt to save others' lives. He was Arthur Lesley Brown, who crashed on the side of the Weaver near Shrewbridge (close to where there is now a parking area) on 14th January 1944. Had he landed in the town much would undoubtedly have been destroyed by fire. Every year a wreath of poppies is laid on Remembrance Sunday on the monument close to the crash site.

NESTON

A busy residential town, but seek out the old coast line of the Dee. There are a few remnants of the old quay from which ships left for Dublin after the Dee became too silted. The silts built up at Neston too and its trade was taken over by Parkgate before moving to Liverpool. Near the 18th century Harp pub, a reminder of Irish trade, can be found overgrown slag heaps and abandoned workings. It is still close enough to the water to be cut off by high tides occasionally.

Emma Hart was baptised on 12th May 1765, the daughter of the village blacksmith, who died when she was a child. She and her mother made a living carrying coal from the mines here to sell, but she was recognised as a beauty and left to be painted by the finest artists - especially Romney - before being lost as the stake in a card game to Sir William Hamilton whom she married. He became Ambassador to the court at Naples but was more interested in the ruins of Pompeii and classical art. It was there she met and fell in love with Nelson, and outraged London when she lived with him in the same house as her husband - who by all accounts was happy with the arrangement and continued his classical studies. Ironically some of Hamilton's old collection found its way to the Lady Lever Gallery along with a portrait of her with Vesuvius smoking in the distance.

NETHER ALDERLEY

The old churchyard has a story of grave robbers who were captured in the act. The JPs could not find an appropriate law under which to prosecute until someone noticed one corpse was wearing a wedding ring taken from the corpse and the charge was theft. In a moat stands Chorley Hall, the oldest inhabited house in Cheshire, of 14th century date. A finely decorated Tudor half-timbered wing is next to it but they were not originally joined. You can see it from the road but it is a lived in home, not open to the public.

An old timber-framed house is the 'Bird and Babby', once an inn called the Stanley Arms. An old story tells of how Thomas Lathom was a sad man as he was one of the richest men in Lancashire but had no son to leave his possessions to. He fathered a son by a local girl, Mary Oscatel, then told his wife of a dream in which he saw an eagle bring them the son they both wanted. He arranged for the boy to be placed near an eagle's nest and took her that way pretending to find the boy. On his deathbed he confessed all and the estates went to his daughter who was married to one of the Stanleys, ancestor of the Earls of Derby, who adopted an eagle and child as their crest. There is no truth in the story and the crest was probably derived from classical carvings of the eagle which stole the infant Ganymede to be cup bearer to the gods.

The real story is almost as unbelievable. Thomas Stanley was given many honours, including the town of Northwich by Richard III, and became second husband to Margaret Beaufort, mother of Henry Tudor. Shakespeare tells us, he stood by until he could tell who was winning the Battle of Bosworth before joining in and crowning Henry VII on the battlefield. The Alderley branch of the family were descended from his second son, John. When the Weaver estates were left to an heiress Henry Tudor made Stanley her guardian and he promptly arranged a marriage ensuring a second important estate for the family. It was the descendants of this marriage who lived at Alderley.

Their country house burnt down but the park contains the ICI research HQ. A pleasant memory is kept by the family: letters published by Nancy Mitford, one of the famous sisters, who were related to the Stanleys. They have a mortuary chapel in the churchyard, and monuments with effigies to Victorian members including a lovely brass portrayal of Lady Stanley in a crinoline surrounded by her children in the church. There is an unusual family pew suspended above an aisle looking like a box at the opera. It originated in a dispute with the Fitton family, who were left with the ground floor while the Stanleys built their own superior accommodation upstairs.

NEW BRIGHTON

In the 1830s steam ferries made it possible to cross the Mersey in some safety and a 'New Brighton' was planned to be like the original, a place for the wealthy and fashionable from Lancashire to cross to and enjoy sea bathing. It was originally intended to have large 'villa' houses for the industrial new rich.

However, it started to attract ordinary Liverpool people and to cater for them when the ferry came to the end of a pier. It soon established fairgrounds and all sorts of gaudy seaside attractions including the 'Ham and Eggs Parade' where cheap food could be purchased, but it was also a place which attracted pickpockets and women without morals. The swimming pool was once one of the biggest in the world; able to hold 3,000 bathers and ten times as many who came to watch the beauty contests which were among the most sought after titles on the circuit.

New Brighton is now getting over its reputation as 'the last resort' which it gained as people discovered holidays overseas and now attracts those who come for an afternoon on a sunny day. When last I visited many people were sitting outside the bars enjoying a drink and a meal and others were water skiing and riding jet skis on the river. It once had a tower, higher than Blackpool's, but only the name remains as it was taken down in 1919 having been considered too conspicuous and too close to Liverpool during the war. The base remained and was one of the early venues for the Beatles and other Mersey Beat groups of the 1960s before it burnt down. There is, however, Fort Perch Rock, built in 1826-9, with its lighthouse to guard the entrance to the Mersey. It is now open for the public to walk over the sands and visit.

NORTHWICH

This busy shopping town looks much older than it really is. Many structures in the centre are less than 100 years old. Yet they hark back to a romantic idea of the past, with half timber and carving; look at the dated examples. You will find a 'flapper' and the date of the 1929 'flapper election', when women first voted with full equality. She is above the door of a building society by the Town Bridge.

The shops were built so that they could be jacked up in case of subsidence as the town fell into flooded and disused salt mines, fulfilling a prophesy by the Cheshire prophet Nixon (who always spoke of doom and disaster) that the town would be destroyed by water. Parts of the town were lifted 20 feet in 20 years. The timber frames helped hold the buildings together when the land moved, and inside the walls were covered with tongue and

Town Bridge, Northwich

groove wood - not plaster - to prevent bricks falling on people. Others were made lightweight, simply with planks nailed to wooden frames. Boot's retained the old front while building a modern shop behind, however careless workmen put the decorated panels back in place upside down - the fruits should hang naturally from the top!

Architecturally it is one of the most unusual and interesting towns anywhere. It deserves recognition as it has one of the best Vernacular Revival streets in Britain, but built that way to be functional, not just decorative. In the shopping malls, built in the 1960s, none of the shops are joined to those next door so that slight subsidence of the land can be accommodated by allowing each one to move separately.

It has two swing bridges with interest hidden underneath. They rest on pontoons which float in the water so that they can operate even if the land sinks and are weighted at one end as a cantilever. Two were required by law so that if one was out of action the other could still be used. The half-timbered Brunner Library is, or was, the slowest mobile library in the world, at one time it moved just half an inch a year!

The 16th century Witton church dominates it on a hill. Witton was the area where the salt makers lived and its name is from the Saxon 'Wych Tune' (the town by the salt works). On the roof is a naughty little imp which acts as a down-spout to drain the central part. It should be as well known as the famous 'mannequin' in Brussels as when it rains he answers the call of nature. A white stone with an urn by the Church Street entrance is to James Dean, who was instrumental in forming the 'Showman's Guild'. Northwich was one of the traditional towns where the fairground folk went for the winter. Until his time there had been no organisation of fairs, often a fist fight established who set up where. The Guild still flourishes imposing strict rules about the running of fairgrounds both for the good of the patrons and the people who operate them.

Next to the churchyard is Vickersway Park. There is a little open air collection of odds and ends from the town including carved stones taken from the church when it was restored in the Victorian period and found in the garden of a local house. There is also a large slab of stone with marks left by cracking mud in the Triassic period 200,000 years ago. On it can be spotted footprints of rhynchosaurus, a small reptile not much bigger than a cat. It came from the Weaver Navigation's quarries at Weston.

On the other side of town the spire of the Waterman's Church (see Runcorn) was built for men on barges on the river. It points out where the Roman fort of Condate once was. The Roman word for fort is *castra* and people would talk about the Castra until the name became Castle. No archaeological evidence of a true medieval castle has been found, but from time to time when

Brunner Library, Northwich

houses are demolished for rebuilding archaeologists take the opportunity to excavate. They have traced remains of Roman barracks, defensive ditches and ramparts, pottery kilns and an unusual iron helmet made to resemble a wig with locks of hair hammered out of iron. The view from the end of Waterloo Road, looking over the Weaver Navigation Offices, shows why the Romans chose this spot on the road from Chester, through Manchester to York.

Northwich still remembers the day the Beatles came to town in July 1963. They had been booked to provide dance music at the Memorial Hall on Saturday evening and someone decided it would be good publicity for the dance if they crowned the Carnival Queen that afternoon. In the few weeks between being booked for the hall and their appearance they had topped the pop charts and no one, least of all the police and the committee, were prepared for what happened. Girls from all over the country converged on the park and when the 'fab four' appeared on stage they surged forward. Paul put the crown on upside down before they fled in an old van. That night the hall was beseiged by hundreds of girls who could not get tickets to get inside. The Beatles had been popular before this and there had been frenzy in the dance halls, but this was the first time that a whole town had been taken over in this way. A couple of months later the term 'Beatlemania' was invented. The Beatles appeared several times at the hall, the last time to keep a long standing booking - they played early in the evening and then rushed to London to perform at a packed Royal Albert Hall.

OAKMERE

There are several meres in Cheshire which might have their origins in pockets of ice left by the glaciers. One of them is Oakmere with the Fishpool Inn a reminder that it belonged to Vale Royal Abbey. Overlooking it is Eddisbury Hill (no public access) which was an Iron Age hill fort, destroyed by the Romans then rebuilt by the Saxon Queen Aethelflaeda when she defended Mercia against the Danes. It has remained almost without habitation since. Another Iron Age settlement, on private land, is by the lake side at Oakmere.

A pub with an interesting name, by the Roman road from

Whitchurch to Warrington, is Cabbage Hall. It was built with the profits made by a tailor from reusing off-cuts of fabric, which were known in the trade as cabbage in the 18th century.

OULTON PARK

Oulton Park, the home of the Grey Egerton family, was destroyed by fire in 1926. It was believed that, as it was the year of the General Strike, it may have been arson, but this proved not to be so. There was, however, ill feeling because the timbers supporting a huge lead water tank in the roof collapsed and killed several men who were saving the priceless art treasures. Everyone originally got out alive and many felt it was a pointless loss of life.

The park was occupied by the military, including Americans during the Second World War and the footway in to the park uses a bridge they built while practising for D-Day. The herd of deer were all killed (then eaten!) on Government orders because they got in the way. All the trees on the common have grown since the war as the old trees were cleared for tank practice; it is now a nature reserve. Today the park contains a famous race track which attracts huge audiences. Probably most do not stop to think about the setting which was laid out by William Eames in the 18th century and has some magnificent trees. All that remains to remind us of the house of the Grey Egertons is the arched entrance lodge capped by their three-arrow crest and a monument to John Francis Egerton. He died in India but is remembered by a magnificent Victorian structure with pinnacles, statues and a spire. The wall which was built to keep the deer in and the poachers out was the reason for selecting this place for the track as it stops those who have not paid from watching the races.

For lovers of the quaint, follow the road which follows that wall and look out for a tiny cottage. It is not big enough to be a complete dwelling and must have been part of a cottage two or three times as long, most of which has been demolished, leaving just one room and a loft in a pretty garden like a greeting card. Not far from the Egerton Arms pub is the old pinfold where animals which strayed were kept until the owner paid the fine to get them back.

The old lock up at Over

OVER

The ancient borough was joined to Wharton on the other side of the river when Winsford Urban District was formed in 1894. St Chad's church contains a small fragment of a Saxon cross. It may have been set up to mark a visit by him to what is believed to have been a sort of pagan sacred grove for religious meetings in the forest. It has a formerly circular churchyard which often indicates pagan worship. It is generally considered unlucky to be buried in the shadow of the church, and it was an area usually left for suicides and others who did not deserve the full blessing. So few such burials occurred at Over that the north semi circle is now used as a car park, but it still retains its circular plan with a matching path on the south. To add to its pagan credentials there are several wells. The ancients were convinced that the world was surrounded by water over and under it as well as around it. Rain fell from the sky and if you dug a well you found water. Wells were used for sacrifice - as we still put a coin in a wishing well. Over is the only church in Cheshire to hold a well dressing ceremony, when they are decorated with flowers.

The church was rebuilt in 1543 for Hugh Starkey, Gentleman Usher (similar to Black Rod) to Henry VIII, who has a brass portrait inside. At least there is a brass portrait, but it is believed that faced with two rather battered tombs the picture of the father was placed on the tomb of his son as an 'improvement' in Victorian times. The armour is certainly of the time of Henry VII not VIII. Just to add to the confusion the century of his death is given in Latin numerals as MC (1005) but should be MV for the 1500s. Some suggest it was made in his lifetime, but as he died after the Reformation no one dared (or was bothered to) put the rest of the letters in. Or did someone start, realise their mistake then give up? To add to the confusion some books say he died in 1555, others 1577, and to cap it all it appears he was actually buried at Little Budworth. The father's tomb is now outside and reused for Archdeacon Woods of Middlewich! The old Blue Bell Inn next to it was burned down, but an exact replica was set up and it now serves refreshments, but not alcoholic ones, in the summer.

Legend tells that the Devil was angry with the people from Over so he tried to steal the church which originally stood in the centre of the old village half a mile away. There is an old print showing him in the air, wings outstretched, with the church under his arms, but the monks of Vale Royal Abbey rang the bells and frightened him away:

> And that's the reason why, they say,
> Over Church from Over Town stands
> Distant many roods away,
> Beyond Town Fields in valley low,

Where parishioners from Over go,
And if truth they tell the Devil's own smell
Of brimstone's in it still.

The sulphurous smell actually came from the hundreds of salt factory chimneys which once filled the valley near it. There were probably more industrial chimneys in one tiny area than on any other similar sized spot on earth. From the churchyard you get a glimpse of a lovely legacy of that time. The flash was created when earth collapsed into spaces left by pumping brine from underground to the works and is now a lake where you can watch swans and sailboats.

An intriguing stone cross in the old borough contains a cell beneath its nine steps with a door at the back now blocked up. Despite the mistaken name of Saxon Crossway close to it, the structure is not very ancient and was probably set up when the market was revived in the building next to it in 1840. It was not a success and had closed down by 1858 because a better market by the river in Winsford took away the trade and Lord Delamere purchased the market hall to convert it to a school. The cell was only to hold people overnight before they went to the magistrates court for the Eddisbury Hundred at the Abbey Arms. Lock ups gradually replaced the stocks and pillories during the 19th century. When the first police stations opened they had better and more secure cells and the lock ups went out of use. It was used as a fuel store for the school boilers when I first knew it. The only other market cross with a prison cell inside is at Hinton St Mary in Lincolnshire where the cell was constructed inside the steps of a medieval cross in the 1840s. A closer look shows that the wall is a different type of stone than the steps, and when you could go into it you could see that the inside was of softer stone than the outside which implies that a plain lock up was given a new look as a cross sometime after it was built.

The Court Leet of the Mayor was held in the George and Dragon and anyone caught stealing from the market was kept in the lock up until he could be dealt with by the court. When it was suggested that the ancient mace should be given to the new UDC, Lord Delamere, Lord of the Manor, hit the table at the George with it so hard that he left a dent which can still be seen on the shaft, and marched off to Vale Royal with it. His son eventually sold it to the Council. There are two maces which go before Winsford's Mayor, one the 17th century one of Over and a new Winsford mace made in 1910 and probably unique as it has the coronet of the Prince of Wales and Earl of Chester in place of the crown. Few people realise that when they are seen as a pair they represent Cheshire's old palatine status indicating the townsfolk are loyal to the Earl who was subservient to the Monarch.

The first Lord Delamere gave St John's church so that villagers did not have to go so far, and in the churchyard by the path is a monument to eight people who died in a mill fire in 1874. The oldest was just 32 and was the mother of the youngest, a baby of three months. It was common for mothers to take their baby to work to feed while continuing to earn money. They were caught on the top floor and died when trying to escape through a window; the baby was crushed falling on the cobbles and his aunt died when her dress caught in the window catch.

Grange Lane between Over and Whitegate is hardly used any more, but is an attractive walk past a bluebell wood with a little stream in the valley totally natural and unspoiled. Above it is tall Bark House (also known as Bank House and Bridge End House) and it was there that Robert Nixon was born. No one knows if he ever really existed and there are two versions of the tale; one says he was active at the time of Henry VII and the other at the time of James I.

It is unlikely to have been in the time of James as many of the things he said were going to happen would actually have happened by then as he told of the dissolution of Vale Royal Abbey, and there is no mention of him in the church registers. The first published account of him appeared long afterwards in 1714, which tells how he was surly and hardly able to say more than a few words except when making his prophesies. He foretold his own end for he said he would be taken to the Royal Court and starved to death. The king ordered that he be taken there but be kept in the palace kitchen to prevent any risk of the prophesy coming true. However, Nixon made such a nuisance of himself by pinching food so he would not starve that the cook locked him in a cupboard and forgot about him. As so often in prophesies the action taken to prevent it coming true actually caused it to happen and he died as he said he would, starved to death amidst plenty. There is a Nixon Drive in Over. It is interesting that the house is next to the Boggart Brook, and a boggart is a northern name for a devil, as Nixon is believed to be a nickname indicating 'The Old Nick's Son'.

OVER PEOVER

A long drive through a farmyard brings you to Over Peover, which was the centre of strategic planning during the Second World War. General Patton used the Elizabethan hall as his HQ in this obscure and hidden place. Cheshire was an ideal base and many Americans were stationed in the county awaiting D-Day, so the Germans could not anticipate which way they would move to the coast. The house where the General stayed is open to the public on certain days, but it is the stables that are the more attractive. Built in 1654 they are rich with carvings and plaster work, it is said no other stables in the land can match them. His American flag is in the church where he prayed, and has 48 stars - Alaska and Hawaii were added after his time.

Warriors of times past are to be found in two chapels, rich with monumental effigies like a text book for the study of costume. It is said that Randle Mainwaring was known as 'Randle the Good' and did not want any fuss, just a simple grave outside the church. His wish was granted and then his wife built a chapel to the side allowing her to be buried inside the church, their effigies side by side in an arch in the wall as a compromise. The Mainwaring crest was an ass's head, as legend tells an ancestor's horse was shot in the Crusades. He found a donkey and rode into Jerusalem with the motto 'Onward if I can', declaring if Christ could ride into the city on a donkey so would he.

PARKGATE

Once ships tied up here to sail for Ireland and even further away before trade moved to the Mersey. It had many distinguished visitors including John Wesley and Handel who composed much of the *Hallelujah Chorus* while staying at Mostyn House, which was then an inn, waiting for the winds to change. He was sailing for Dublin where the first performance of the *Messiah* was to be held and he was making the arrangements for it. By the time he returned it was finished and he made his way to Chester where he spoke to the Dean at the Cathedral who introduced him to a local singer and the organist. The latter assured the composer that he could play at sight, whereupon Handel handed them a manuscript with corrections, alterations, crossings out and remarks in German. The poor men did their best but the result was a meaningless mixture of notes. Furious, Handel shouted, 'You said you could play at sight.' 'So I can', replied the organist, 'but not at first sight'.

The sea long since silted at Parkgate. For a time it enjoyed a second life as a seaside place with a large beach of sand. Now instead of sea there is a vast expanse of vegetation but they still sell home-made ice cream and shrimps from shops along the front. Lady Hamilton, who was born at Neston, spent some time sea bathing here for a skin complaint. Of course she did not gain her title or meet Nelson until long after she left. It is a different Nelson, the son of the miniatures artist Albin Burt, who was swept from the deck of the steamer *Prince Regent* in 1822 and who is commemorated in front of a house near where the Neston road joins the front. The name can be seen in black cobbles in the pavement of a house his father used as a summer home as a reminder of his lost son.

 ## PECKFORTON

The castle was built in between 1844 and 1872 for John Tollemache but was too big to live in or even to keep warm. It was mainly used for summer parties but is so well built in medieval style that no real castle can rival it as a film set. Its woods still contain pheasantries, come this way in season and they will wander out to see you. The estate cottages were almost all made new in Victorian times and many still have their privies and pigsties preserved behind as Tollemache was keen that tenants could be as self sufficient as possible.

There is one unexpected animal, the elephant. Actually he is a bit flat and thin, but he is almost large as life, carved from a single block of sandstone with a castle on his back. That served as an elaborate bee hive with glass in the windows through which to watch the bees. Bee castles were quite a feature of Victorian country houses. As the castle is actually made in three separate sections totally separate from the beast and much wider they were probably not originally one structure - it certainly sits awkwardly on the back and you would need a ladder to watch the bees! On the other hand if it was at ground level it would be easy to take honeycomb out by lifting bits off. This fits with the tale that it was moved from another site and perhaps the two parts were only joined then. A mason called Watson working on the castle carved the elephant in his spare time for his garden and it now stands in the middle of a group of estate cottages; if he also made the castle is not known.

 ## PENKETH

Penketh can be seen from afar because of the gigantic cooling towers of Fiddler's Ferry power station, but close to it you will find a pub of the same name which is worth a visit for a charming corner which attempts to recreate the ferry-man's office of long ago. He has his grandfather clock and ships' lights to make sure he does his duty, but would you really rely on a man with so many bottles of ale at his elbow? It is said that the name originates in the family of Viola who operated the ferry but were nicknamed 'fiddlers' for obvious reasons. It is a stretch of the North Mersey with wide mud flats which attract winter birds. In fact although Cheshire has precious little coastline as such it has many havens for wild birds in the two estuaries. The Mersey was according to tradition the crueller of the two demanding a life every seven years, while the Dee was said to give up its dead by shining a mysterious light above the place where the body would be found.

 ## PICKMERE

In the Middle Ages it was the Pike Mere where the fish were taken for the table at Norton Priory on a Friday. Not so long ago it was an inland pleasure resort with fairground, boat rides, a club and refreshment stands. In the days when few had cars, or petrol was on ration, a bus from Manchester to Northwich passed by so people could come out for a few hours in the country.

In the years between the wars the lake became lined by bungalows. Working people either moved out of the towns to retire here or used them as weekend cottages and often built them themselves from scrap materials; many were hardly more than sheds. They were built by people who simply wanted a taste of the country and this was one of many such settlements which people who had served in the First World War set up as an alternative to city life. They wanted little more than camping conditions, but tastes changed with increased car ownership and a widening of horizons following air holidays abroad. Exciting theme parks took over from a simple row on a lake. As the fairground and day trippers declined the land was sold to developers. The bungalows were, fortunately, surveyed before they were demolished to record a lost way of life in a more uncomplicated age.

PLEMSTALL

You turn from a very ordinary piece of the A56 into a residential street and then follow a long narrow lane over the fields. At the end is nothing but a church and a farm in a lonely spot by the Gowy. It has a tale to tell; for Pledgemund, a saintly hermit here, was called from his island in the Gowy marshes to become Archbishop to King Alfred the Great. He was the inspiration behind a revival of arts and religion in Wessex which saw Bibles copied and given to every monastery in the land - many had no books until then. The church can still be flooded and recently a wedding had to be moved to another church because Plemstall was under water. It is not much higher than the river and it is not hard to imagine that only a foot or two of water more would make this an island again as the river flows on both sides. St Pledgemund's well was decorated by those wanting help, who tied a strip of fabric in the traditional way to the railings and trees. This is an ancient ritual and has origins in pagan times when leaving a strip of your clothing was like leaving part of your identity.

Outside there is the large vault of the Hurlestons, with a table tomb above it. On the sides are carved skeletons, reminders that all people must die; other similar 'cadavar' (corpse) tombs exist at Gawsworth, and at St Mary's and St John's in Chester. They have scythes and hour glasses to show that they were cut down when their time had run out. If you count the ribs you will find one is supposed to be male and is lacking the mythical 'spare rib'. An attractive addition to the site has been the establishment of a wildflower meadow. Originally planted with native flowers, they have now self seeded and are thriving in the rich soil of the flood plain.

Part of the parish, Pickton, is worth including here for the description given by Dr Ormerod around 1816: 'In road, appearances and inhabitants, it may safely be said to present a complete picture of barbarism' - today it is a pleasant group of mellow old buildings.

PLUMLEY

Only part of Holford Hall survives. It was used by Lady Mary Cholmondeley (nee Holford) as a retirement home after settling Cholmondeley, Vale Royal and Knight's Grange onto her three sons. The style of architecture looks as though this house was built when she was still young, and before she married and embarked on her house building and collecting. What is left is reached by a delightful bridge with seats part way across the moat. Around it the chemical works drill holes and extract the brine then fill the space with chemical waste. Before they started to do this, between the wars, there were plans to tip waste in the moat. Part of the hall was taken down because it was not used and so was the old mill. The wood from both was sold during a coal strike for use as fuel. Now what is left is delightfully looked after as a private dwelling. Plumley has the Smoker Inn and a group of old timber-framed cottages by a turning from the busy Manchester to Chester road. To find Holford Hall you take the next turning on the Northwich side along a cul de sac, but it is a private home and not open to the public, so do not leave the road.

Plumley Station hit the headlines a few years ago when there were plans to close it but it was found to be the most widely used village station in the land, with people coming from all parts of the country. The reason was that the home of pop star Gary Barlow was next to it and his fans came to try to catch a glimpse of him and the group 'Take That', which used a recording studio joined to the house. The station buildings are now a centre for management training, but have been restored to their pre-war appearance.

PORT SUNLIGHT

It needs no introduction and was the creation, from 1888, of Lord Leverhulme who started his working life slicing carbolic soap in Bolton - the contraption he used is still on show - and then made a fortune by selling soap ready shaped, wrapped, nicely scented and called 'Sunlight'. He built the factory and a wonderful village for his workers where no two groups of houses are the same and although it is named after the soap, few workers' homes of his day made better use of the sunlight. It was a total contrast to the dark, monotonous terraced housing which had gone before. Famous architects built the homes in the midst of open gardens and allotments - some now converted to car parks. It became a fossilised piece of the taste of the early 20th century, yet it influenced the style of many inter-war council housing developments which followed the same principle and became known as 'garden cities'. He continued his love affair with the period of the Arts and Crafts movement, and pre-Raphaelites, long after the First World War changed art and architecture to a more brutal modernism.

The Lady Lever Gallery is entirely of his taste; it is one of the wonders of the North and described as Merseyside's Taj Mahal. Yet few outside the world of art know of it or expect to find such a thing in an 'industrial village'. Many who come expecting to see a few old fashioned paintings in a dull municipal gallery are astonished to find one of the world's great collections of beautiful things, including fine craftsmanship in pottery, furniture and sculpture. It is this unexpected aspect that earns so grand a building a place in a book of the unexpected. It contains countless hidden gems to discover.

Perhaps the item which sums up Port Sunlight best is the War Memorial, a fabulous piece of the 'New Sculpture' which Leverhulme loved so much. Bronze soldiers stand ready to defend women and children in this most peaceful of spots. He was keen on military training and encouraged his men to go to war in 1914. Many never returned and slowly his lovely village became filled with aged widows or couples who had lived here from the start but were too old to work. For a time it was almost desolate and you seldom heard the laughter of a child. Then changes were made allowing residents to move into smaller, more appropriate accommodation and people were allowed to buy houses who did not work in the soap works as long as they agreed to recognise the unique nature of the place. Now the village is alive again.

Leverhulme made a unique contribution to world affairs too, for he gave Lancaster House in London as a suitable and dignified setting where leaders could get together on neutral territory to discuss affairs. It has often seen peaceful rather than warlike ends to conflicts.

 ## POTT SHRIGLEY

A little hill village in a pretty wooded setting where several brooks meet, with an old church which contains yet another possible Cheshire Cat (see Brimstage and Grappenhall entries). Its founder specified that the priest should keep 'no hawk nor hound' which would have been a temptation hard to resist in these moors in an age when hunting was considered an essential for gentlemen. Beyond, the road into Derbyshire has another culinary sounding name in Bakestonedale. Special smooth stones were quarried here which were incorporated into the hearths of cottages long ago. In the days of the Corn Laws in the 19th century these moors were used to produce oats in great quantities. They were used to mix a porridge which was turned to bake on the hot bakestone to make oatcakes, which made a good substitute for bread. They could either be wrapped around sandwich fillings or dried and dipped into stews or 'cheese dips' made by melting dry cheese scraps in hot milk; nourishing food for the poor of the industrial towns. If Marie Antoinette really said the poor of France should eat cake when the price of bread became too much is not known, but the poor of the North of England certainly ate and enjoyed oatcakes as the staple of their diet.

 ## POYNTON

Just when you think you are starting to know Cheshire it springs a surprise on you. Such is Poynton, for it is an old coal mining community in a county where you do not expect to find one, though coal has been mined in east Cheshire, particularly around Stalybridge, and also in the Wirral. Its old bits have a solid feel with rows of former miners' cottages around a four branched lamp-post in the centre which once doubled as a drinking fountain with water going through different troughs for people, horses and a little one for dogs. Now they are used as planters for flowers.

Although the coal mine closed down in 1935 the old railway inclines along which coal trucks ran have become walks to the canal from the disused station, which is an access point to the Middlewood Way. This follows the track of the former Marple to Macclesfield line and was sold by British Railways for just £1 to be converted. You can still take a train ride in Poynton though, as a miniature railway with a station, signals and a collection of railway relics is a feature of the local garden centre.

 ## PRESTBURY

Splendidly well known and affluent, the churchyard has a couple of sad stories on its graves:

> Beneath this stone lies Edward Green,
> Who for cutting stone famous was seen,
> But he was sent to apprehend
> One Joseph Clark of Kerridge End,
> For stealing deer from Esquire Downes
> When he was shot and died of the wounds.

Presumably it was his year to serve as parish constable. Kerridge was noted for the stones which broke into flat 'flags' and were extensively used for floors and roofing in this part of Cheshire. There is also the melodramatic:

> Well might the thunder rend the air
> To see such monsters dwelling there;
> Thrice helpless child, thus doomed to roam
> And leave your every friend at home.

It records how in 1721 eight year old Francis Rathbone lost her way home from a nearby shop. Shunned by everyone she met she wandered far away and was found dead under a hedge at

Over Peover. In the churchyard are a Saxon cross, a Norman chapel and the old church, with the old priest's house, a splendid black and white building, serving as a bank opposite. Tradition says that when the Puritan rector was 'ejected' from the church on the return of Charles II he continued to preach a rival Puritan sermon to his congregation from the balcony.

PUDDINGTON

Two men from the Hall died in Chester Castle. Father Pleasington ministered to the family here when Catholics were allowed to worship only in private. In 1689 Titus Oates told of a Catholic plot to oust the new Protestant King and Queen, William and Mary, and the priest was taken to Chester Castle to be hanged, drawn and quartered. The quarters were sent back with instructions that one part was to be displayed on each corner of the Hall. It is claimed that he was buried in Burton churchyard, but when what was supposed to be his grave was opened in 1962 it was empty. The gravestone was taken to St Winefride's Catholic church in Neston as a memorial. In 1714 William Massey, also Catholic, went to fight for the Old Pretender at Preston, but fled after the defeat. His horse swam over the Mersey with him, but died exhausted near the gate to Puddington. He was captured and taken to Chester Castle where it is believed the conditions and cold weather killed him.

The Old Hall was given a coat of pebble dash rendering in an attempt to preserve it so that at first it does not look old enough for such a history. An unusual survival for this area is an 18th century dovecote amongst its old farm buildings.

The dovecote dates from the time before frozen food and ensured a meat supply through the winter. Farm animals and poultry were reduced to a minimum by autumn killing so only a few lived through the worst months when food was short to start breeding in the spring. Doves and pigeons foraged for scraps of food that they found over a large area and always returned to their own little 'pigeon hole'. This was the origin of pigeon races. However, they laid eggs regularly which could be harvested by simply climbing to each hole and when the time came the birds themselves were sitting waiting ready to be put into pies or the cooking pot. As there was better winter forage in Cheshire than in most other counties, the importance of pigeon meat was less and it is unusual to find dovecotes here.

RAINOW

Formerly an industrial village, Rainow is now a pretty area with wide views and paths along flagged pavements over the fields which were once trodden by pack-horses and the clogs of workers on their way to the factories. Its name is said to originate in ravens rather than the weather. The Hole House at the end of Sugar Lane is specially interesting. James Mellor who lived there in the middle of the 19th century came from a manufacturing family, but lived as a gentleman with his own religious beliefs. He followed the teachings of Emmanuel Swedenborg, Swedish scientist/theologian, and built his own private chapel and preached his own services. Mellor wanted to create a reflection of heaven in his garden, which he laid out with quotes from the Bible carved in stone. It had a route which included impressions of features in Bunyan's *Pilgrim's Progress*; including the Slough of Despond, the Hill of Difficulty and finally his chapel as the Celestial City. A strange structure in the garden is the 'Howling House': where an aeolian harp was hung. When the doors were opened the wind blew through the strings creating sound from fresh air. They were not so rare as you might think in an age when nature was the inspiration for philosopy The garden is open on certain days in the summer.

The misty hills around Rainow, especially the long lane which leads to the delightful Rainalow, can evoke ideas of mysticism and magic. So it is not surprising to read that in 1656 after several people in the district were taken mysteriously ill and died Ellen, the wife of John Beach, and Anne, the wife of John Osbaston, were accused of 'certayn artes' and 'wicked and devilish actes'. They were taken to the castle at Chester, tried at the Michaelmas assizes and executed on 8th October. Their funerals were recorded in the registers at St Mary on the Hill, the church adjoining the castle, which is now used as an education centre. They were buried in the ditch between the castle and the churchyard rather than on consecrated ground.

They were the victims of a mania which gripped England in the early 17th century, when King James I was convinced that witches had tried to drown him as he sailed to take the English throne. Innocent people were forced to claim that they had sailed in sieves to sink his ship, which inspired a line in *The Scottish Play*. James wrote a book called *Demonology* and passed acts to control witchcraft. With such royal patronage there was little wonder that if anything went wrong, any old or odd character was at once accused of witchcraft, tortured to confess and then executed. The Rainow Women and another from Eaton who was executed at the same time, fared better than some witches in 17th century Chester. An account published in a newspaper of 1649 records witch burning in the city: 'two this day, 11 tomorrow, 25 were burnt on the 14th'. There are few records of actual witch burning in this country as that was usually associated with Catholic countries where they were tried for 'heresy' and burnt. In England execution by hanging was the more usual and this seems to have been the fate of the two women from Rainow about whom we know nothing more.

REASE HEATH

A splendid Victorian mansion which was once the Cheshire School of Agriculture, but is now a more general college. The hall itself has woodwork and stained glass in High Victorian manner, and there are immaculately cared for grounds with a lake full of water-lilies and a lawn sweeping down to it. You would expect nothing less in a place that teaches horticulture, and a maze has been planted for visitors to explore. It is a place to come in spring on one of its lambing days. All the college's skills are used to try to ensure they are born when visitors are allowed to watch or see the new ones and help feed them. For hygiene reasons there is a glass-fronted observation chamber from which to watch cattle milked. There is also the chance to buy real Cheshire cheese, fresh eggs and other farm products from the shop. It is still a college which is predominantly for agriculture but also offers short courses and one of the delights is that almost everything served at meal times was produced within a few yards of where you eat it.

RINGWAY

Older people still refer to Ringway Airport, but it has long been known as Manchester International Airport and one of the busiest in the world. It had an ancient chapel which was made new in 1894 and is now redundant, and its old inn attracts many people on a sunny day to watch the aircraft come and go; often one every couple of minutes. The pub is now known to all as 'The Romper' but originally it was the 'Lion Rampant'. Because of the way the painter had depicted the lion it was soon known as the 'Romping Kitling' (kitten) and that name was adopted officially.

Around it are modern roads and the buildings of a great airport have taken over what old guide books tell us was a little out of the way village. The original aerodrome was built in 1937-8 and during the war was used to train parachute troops who practised by dropping into the open space of Tatton Park, or doing water drops into Rostherne Mere. It experienced its own little war recently when protesters tried to prevent the second runway taking over the landscape of Cheshire, including the National Trust woods at Styal. Two ancient half-timbered buildings at Mobberley stood in the way, but were completely dismantled and re-erected on a different site well away from the planes which are now as much a feature of this part of the country as the black and white cows. Close to the runway, an inscription on the end of a barn records how the farm was rebuilt after a hurricane in the 18th century.

ROMILY

Romily has a pretty little chapel dedicated to St Chad which gave its name to the area of Chadkirk. It is one of several places in the county with his name which might indicate that he preached there. The origins of the chapel are uncertain but it was abandoned when a new church was built in 1865 to accommodate the many workers who had moved to mills in what had once been the quiet wooded Goyt valley. It had never been a very well attended church because it was remote. At one time it it was used as a stable, at another the Nonconformists worshipped here. Eventually in 1973 the local authority took over responsibility for it. Since then it has been restored and taken on a new life as a community centre. Its religious origins have not been forgotten and several contemporary religious works of art have been added.

🍇 ROSTHERNE

Rostherne is only a short distance from the entrance to Tatton Park, but many who go there miss this gem. Some houses were built for people from the former village in Tatton Park. Rostherne has a square of houses with backyards with walls too high to gossip over as Lady Egerton hated gossip. Some books say there are no backdoors, but they have them to reach the yards. Its church is older with a splendid setting overlooking the mere and has memories of Adam Martindale who was Puritan vicar here until 'ejected' on the Restoration. When villagers set up a maypole he preached a dismal sermon saying how it was in honour of the 'strumpet Flora' in pagan Rome. His wife and servant went one better and cut it down in the night.

The beautiful memorial in Rostherne church

A legend of the church tells how a bell fell into the nearby mere because a workman swore when it would not move properly - the same tale is told at Combermere. A mermaid is said to ring it once a year. Today you must not go near the water as it is a nature reserve, but watch from the churchyard in season and you will see flocks of migrating birds coming in to roost at dusk even if you don't see her! The churchyard has a 17th century gate with a weight so it closes automatically. The area next to the wall is fenced off. According to tradition the bachelor Lord Egerton found a couple on the grass there and set up the fence so that such activity could not happen again!

Inside the church is a memorial in white marble to Charlotte Lucy Egerton. Records say she died of a bronchial infection at Tatton in 1845. But local tradition tells that she drowned in the mere on the eve of her wedding and is shown wearing her wedding dress. She is depicted by Westmacott as if asleep, while above her kneels a life size, free standing, angel, wings outspread. No monument in Cheshire is more lovely or worth seeing or so much epitomises Victorian sentimentality and belief.

 ## RUNCORN

I sometimes think everything in Runcorn is hidden! You come to it with no problem but once you get on the Expressway you always seem to be going the wrong way or you don't see the sign for where you want until it is too late to turn.

It is a busy modern town with a few quiet corners to impress. Come on a sunny day with a gentle breeze and find the Waterman's Church surrounded by sparkling water at Weston Point. It was one of three built by the Weaver Navigation Trustees who were responsible for trade on the river as a reaction to the 'South Sea Bubble'. The Government only allowed them to give the standard rate of interest and all other profits were to be used for the good of the county, and there were plenty of profits from the salt trade. They built Chester Castle and Knutsford Gaol and three churches with their schools where boat people could attend no matter where they were on a Sunday. The one at Winsford was demolished, at Northwich it dominates the town, but here it seems to float on shimmering water where the Weaver Navigation, the Ship Canal and the Mersey meet.

The Waterman's Church, Runcorn

Runcorn was the product of water transport, but the flight of locks which the Duke of Bridgewater built to take his canal into the Mersey, and then persuaded the Trent and Mersey to also use - at a charge - have been filled in. The Duke of Bridgewater's canal passes through the grounds of Norton Priory. Richard Brooke the owner held up construction for a time, objecting. In a pincer military-style move the canal was built from Manchester and from Runcorn until only his park stood between and public pressure made him give way. The house has long gone but you can now explore the excavated ruins of the ancient priory and a museum containing information and finds, also visit the old walled garden and summer house, a delight at most times of the year.

When the new town was first planned they decided that it needed 'roots' and a small excavation was commissioned. That was to lead to the largest excavation of a monastic site anywhere in Britain following modern principals of excavation. Besides laying out the plan of the church and the buildings around the cloister where the canons lived, excavators found a pit used to cast a bell, and local industry enabled an exact copy to be cast;

you can ring it yourself today. They excavated a kiln used to make the tiles for the floor and the largest area of medieval tiles ever discovered in Britain. Also on show is the largest medieval carving to survive in Britain, a gigantic St Christopher, a much bigger version of the carving on Great Budworth church tower, showing him crossing a river with fish swimming between his legs and the Christ child on his back. This is a reminder that the monks operated a ferry over the Mersey long before the bridges over it were ever imagined.

 ## SALE

Many modern towns in Cheshire have their older counterparts, Crewe was in Church Coppenhall, Ellesmere Port was Netherpool, Over is old Winsford and Sale's hidden old corner is around the church of Ashton on Mersey.

Sale is bounded by the Mersey and its name is from the Saxon for willows - there are a few by the river still. It has a night club which is, surprisingly, the feature of special interest to the collector of oddities. Originally it was a cinema called the Pyramid and has gone through many uses including a bingo hall and a dance hall. The advent of the cinema, especially the 'talkies', coincided with a renewed interest in ancient Egypt, particularly after Tutankhamun's tomb was opened. There was a rash of films showing sultry Egyptian 'vamps', and women wore slinky dresses, head gear and even eye shadow (unheard of before) as well as sequins and diamante to capture the Egyptian look. The cinema was built in Egyptian style with Art Deco details in 1933. It was closer to the Mersey than the Nile and stood in the middle of a row of shops. But who cared? It was a place to fantasise and dream of a sultry night in the desert.

Sale once had its own mummy. Miss Beswick, an elderly patient of Dr Thomas White, was afraid of being buried alive. She arranged that he would inherit everything if he ensured that she was not buried. This he did, keeping her preserved body in a grandfather clock case with a white velvet curtain over the glass. Every year, in front of witnesses, he drew the curtain back to look at her face. When he died the 'Manchester Mummy' became a curio at the Manchester Museum, until the University decided to get rid of all curiosities and just maintain a teaching collection.

She was eventually buried in an unmarked grave in Harpurhey Cemetery in 1868, 111 years after she died.

White maintained a museum in his house at The Priory where another famous relic was the supposed skeleton of Higgins, Knutsford's highwayman. It was said to be the one still on display in Manchester Museum. When I contacted them suggesting they used the skull for one of their famous facial reconstructions they noticed that the one now on display is a modern Indian female, evidently put there to replace a dirty old one. There are three tales about what happened after the execution. One says he was hanged, cut down and buried in the north side of the churchyard - the part reserved for criminals. However, there is no mention of a burial in the church registers. Another is that he was buried in unconsecrated ground. The third claims his body was taken to a Doctor Cruikshank, to be used for instructing his medical students including the young Dr White who inherited it. The body showed signs of still being alive but the doctor carried on with the dissection. Certainly the writer de Quincy wrote of Dr White's skeleton of a highwayman in the 18th century. Researches into the history of the Manchester Museum also found references to a skeleton of a highwayman there during the 19th century. He would not be the only criminal whose skeleton was in a museum; Oxford and Bury St Edmunds both still show them. He remains as elusive in death as he was in life.

SALTERSFORD

There are two, one a tunnel on the Trent and Mersey, notable as one of the first canal tunnels from which it is impossible to see light at both ends because it was constructed in sections. The other is an area of high moorland near the border with Derbyshire where tracks used by pack-horses from the salt towns meet. In the middle of the moors is Jenkyn Chapel, built in 1733 for the ease of worshippers who tended their farms in these drystone walled fields. Before the repeal of the Corn Laws in the 1840s oats, peas, beans and other hardy crops were grown on such land to feed a growing population as cheap imported food was not allowed. It looks more like a house with a strange little tower and a chimney for fires in winter.

Beware if you decide to drive, the narrow lanes between the

Sandbach's 'other' Saxon crosses

walls were not intended for cars; it is almost impossible to see vehicles coming and space to pass is not provided. Take a warning about travelling in bad weather too. In 1735 John Turner set out in heavy snow to spend Christmas with his family, but never arrived. When his frozen body was found just one single woman's shoe print was seen in the snow beside it. The place is marked by a stone by the road set up by his relative who built the 'pilgrim's'garden at Rainow.

SANDBACH

It comes alive on Thursday when a large market is held. It is suggested that the Sandbach crosses were set up to mark the marriage of Peada (pronounced Pe-ar-da) of Mercia to a Northumbrian princess, who brought four priests with her to start the work of converting Mercia as she had refused to live in a pagan land. Perhaps the taller one is for Peada and the shorter one for his wife. Certainly one cross shows four men diligently walking somewhere. One was St Chad who was the first Bishop of Mercia and settled at Lichfield. It is presumed that Sandbach might have been a centre for preaching for a group of priests to travel from on missionary journeys.

The two crosses are well known, but a small group of stones

are now placed separately by the church tower, which is interesting as it has a path through it. The crosses were broken in Puritan times and restored by the historian George Ormerod in 1816. We know he searched far and wide, all over Cheshire for bits of crosses, and there is nothing to prove all these pieces were in Sandbach in Saxon times. Indeed, some came from around Tarvin and Tarporley where we have records that several tall decorated crosses were destroyed by John Bruen in the early 17th century. Are these bits of those crosses?

SANDIWAY

The round tower in the centre of a dual carriageway here excites imagination, it is all that is left of a decorative lodge at the entrance to Vale Royal Park. The Blue Cap Hotel retains the name of a hound who was so fast that he had to wear a lead collar to keep him at the speed of the others as hounds must hunt as a pack not on their own. He won a race against 'Wanton', the pride of the Quorn Hunt, and 500 guineas for his owner, John Smith Barry of Marbury Hall. There are two lanes with 'sporting' memories; in Kennel Lane the Cheshire hounds have their home and Bluecap's monument is now there even though he was buried behind the hotel. In the 1950s the landlord wanted to get rid of it, so it was moved to save it. Close to Cockpit Lane many clay pipes in the form of a cock's claw were found and are now in the County Museums Collections. The village was the home of the architect John Douglas who designed many of the fine houses and the church which are now part of a conservation area.

At Bryn the old chapel has become private dwellings, but retains a memory of a very strange man. He was James Crawford, who was too old to continue working as a farm labourer when he met the founders of the Primitive Methodists. They agreed to give him a small sum as the first paid minister of the new denomination. People flocked to hear 'the old man of the forest' and then told of the wonderful visions they had at Bryn. Then it was found that 'the Rustic Mystic' was using 'magic mushrooms' and the drug-induced visions were often accompanied by frolics in the forest. He and his 'Magic Methodists' were promptly unchurched in 1813 so the Primitive's first paid minister was the first to be thrown out.

SAUGHALL

A picturesque village with a memory of a strange woman. In 1668 she was exhibited 'at the sign of the Swan near Charing Cross', being then 72 years old. When she had been 28 she started to be troubled with 'an excrescence . . .like to a Wen' which grew on her head. This apparently turned to a pair of horns, which she shed from time to time. Examples of the horns were said to have been presented to the Ashmolean Museum and the British Museum - that did not actually exist in her lifetime but it later gained a painting supposedly showing her. That portrait shows a profile, but the horn does not look at all convincing and is more as though she is wearing some sort of hair slide. It is not improbable that her details were added to an old portrait of someone else to make it appear more valuable. The Ashmolean once possessed an engraving based on this, except that in making the copy it has been reversed. The engraver has let his imagination and knowledge of the story turn the hair slide into two horns.

None of the horns seem to have survived so that modern DNA testing could have told us if they really were human or animal's horns and a complete hoax. The Ashmolean Museum in 1983 published an account of the woman which concluded that they were 'cutaneous horns' made up of layers of dry skin cells which sometimes grow from a wart or scar, and are not uncommon on people or animals, but seldom reach this size. Perhaps this explains why they have not survived for if they were just dried cells and not real horns they may simply have crumbled away. At that time there was a great interest in curiosities of all kinds and scientific books included such strange things as deformed animals along with descriptions of rare plants and birds. It was the sort of thing which would have attracted interest in an age which viewed nature and curiosities in a different way than we do today.

 # SHOCKLACH

The castle which once capped the mound here has long vanished, as have all the Norman castles which once defended the Dee valley. The earthworks remain as does the little chapel of

St Edith, on opposite sides of the road north of the village. At the end of a lane, the church has a huge Norman doorway with its half-round arch almost filling one side of the tiny nave. The two little bells in a bellcote were once rung by chains which hung outside. Local people came rushing one night to see what the commotion was about when they heard them ringing in the darkness. They found to their amusement or disgust, depending on their sense of humour, that a joker had tied hay to the chains and a cow was happily munching. The other Norman castles were at Dodleston, Pulford, Aldford, Malpas and Oldcastle, but all were abandoned after a short time as the border was pushed to contain Flint and Denbighshire by the 13th century.

 ## SHOTWICK

There is an old story of how a Green Knight apeared one Christmas at Camelot and challenged King Arthur to do as he did the following Christmas at the Green Chapel, but Sir Gawain asked to stand in his place. Then the Knight cut off his own head and walked out with it! Next year Gawain set out as he had promised and crossed the old ford on the sands of Dee from Wales into Cheshire and into a forest. He found a castle where he was tempted to stay awhile as the Green Chapel was not far away, promising to tell of anything he took. While the knight of the castle went out to hunt, Gawain stole a kiss from his wife the first night but told his host, the second he took two kisses and reported it, before deciding that if he was about to die it was pointless not to enjoy more and keep quiet. When the host returned this time he recognised it was the Green Knight back from a fox hunt and he threw the skin on the floor. Gawain was not killed although his throat was skimmed by the knight's sword. All this links with the facts known about the body found in Lindow Moss near Wilmslow. He had been killed in winter by being garotted and having his throat cut. Mistletoe pollen was found in his lungs - of course mistletoe and kisses go together. The only clothing on the body was a strip of fox skin around an arm! Scholars believe that the story embodies much of ancient mythology going back to the times of Lindow Man.

The story was written for one of the Massey family in the Middle Ages, and they had land in this area by the ancient ford over which Edward I's armies marched into Wales. It was an ancient route used by salt traders which avoided the narrow bridge at Chester and passed through the old forest of Wirral. Was it an 'in the know' gesture by the scribe to thinly disguise Shotwick Castle? However, on the other side of the Dee the story lives on in the unique pub name of 'Sir Gawain and the Green Knight' at Connah's Quay.

There are two Shotwick Lanes leading from the A550, one goes near to the castle, the other just to the quaint village with a picturesque collection of old houses, farm buildings and cobblestones. The churchyard is filled with stones toppled in all directions as if the result of an earthquake, and the walls of the porch are covered in grooves where arrows were sharpened in the past. There are so many one imagines all Edward's invading army sharpening up for battle. Administratively Cheshire stops at the old river's edge not far from the church, and between the church and the water are a couple of miles of Wales; known as Sealand, but totally separate from this hidden village.

SIDDINGTON

Visit at Harvest Festival and its black painted beams are enriched by numerous corn dollies made by local countryside expert Raymond Rush and shown off to perfection. They are essentially pagan symbols, made from the last corn gathered from the field and kept to contain the corn spirit until the fresh crop grew the following year. A fashion I have noted over the last couple of years in the fields is to make a figure of the modern huge rolls of hay with one on its side with eyes and a smile on top and hay bales hung to act as arms. A sign of an evolving countryside.

The heavy roof of Kerridge slabs caused problems for the church which had to be cased in brick in the early 19th century, but it is painted to show where the hidden beams are. By the tower is an unusual looking grave with what looks like a pile of stones. It was set up for a stoker on the railways by his friends in tribute to a life's work and represents a pile of coal. The vicar apparently objected that it was not appropriate, possibly associating stoking with the fires of Hell. The friends set it up in the middle of the night and the vicar relented as it would be too much trouble to move.

SPURSTOW

An old signpost used to say:

> If you are troubled with saw or flaw
> This is the way to Spurstow Spa

with:

> If all your troubles you've left in the lurch
> This is the way to Bunbury Church

You can still find Spurstow Spa on modern OS maps with the additional information that it is saline, however it is totally overgrown and almost impossible to see. Tested by chemists its water was found to contain Epsom salts, probably from chemicals in the sandstone. It might once have cured an upset stomach or hangover and its powers got exaggerated. There were other healing wells. Somewhere in this area was the Wistlebitch Well where in the 17th century wonderful cures were said to result from taking the waters; it was something like a local Lourdes but without religious links. Crutches and walking sticks were said to be left by the lame who could walk after taking the water. The Rev William Cole who took a dip in another healing well in 1757 records it was so cold he could hardly stay in the water for a minute. Perhaps the cold was sufficient to make any hypochondriac gently lowered into the waters quickly gain enough strength to scramble out again and declare a miracle cure!

STALYBRIDGE

The town has a hidden treasure trove of art, Bramley Radcliffe put together a personal collection which included Renaissance art and antiquities from Egypt, Greece and Rome. In recent years the collections have been kept in store as the gallery space at the library has been used for temporary exhibitions of modern art. With a growing interest in such personal collections and lottery grants, perhaps Stalybridge should look again at how best to display the collection.

Stalybridge is still very much a mill town but has one thing for those who seek oddities. There is a blue plaque on The Old Thirteenth Cheshire Astley Volunteer Rifleman Corps Inn, which tells us that it is the longest pub name in Britain. The 'Volunteers' were a sort of Victorian 'Dad's Army' and there were several 'Volunteers' or 'Riflemen' pubs close to where they trained. Usually local landowners were responsible for training them and even providing the uniforms. They often styled themselves as Colonel or Captain not because of genuine military service but because of their command of volunteers. The movement started with the expected invasion by Napoleon III in the middle of the 19th century but in most places ended when the members joined up to fight in the 1914-18 war.

STOAK

Writing at the start of the 19th century, George Ormerod said of Stoke it was 'a collection of ragged and filthy hovels scattered around the church'. Of course his history of Cheshire is entirely devoted to the great families for he was a lawyer involved in the technicalities of inheritances and family trees. Not for Ormerod was there any interest - let alone delight - in the pretty country cottage or pleasures of an old inn. An old rhyme said that:

> In Stoke there are few good folk,
> In Stanney hardly any.

Today the M53 and M56 have a busy interchange only yards from the old church. The village is no longer ragged and filthy. They say that the Devil moved the stones for the church from the original site at Stanney and it is still largely surrounded by fields with a farm for company. The church was rebuilt in 1827, but has the stump of an ancient cross in the churchyard and a one-fingered clock on the tower; one was sufficient in the less hurried days when it was built.

STOCKPORT

On Christmas morning, the bells traditionally ring out the tune of Stockport, 'Christians awake salute the happy morn'.

A visitor some 250 years ago left his feelings written with a diamond ring in a window at the long demolished White Lion Inn:

> If traveller, good treatment be thy care,
> A comfortable bed and wholesome fare,
> A modest bill and a diverting host,
> Neat maid and ready waiter - quit this coast.
> If dirty doings please; at Stockport lie,
> The girls, O frowzy frights, here with their mothers vie.

If you venture there in spite of the warning you should look out the unusual air-raid shelters carved from the rock during the Second World War and kept as a heritage attraction. People have carved into the soft rock to make stores etc for generations. You might find it hard to spot the River Mersey in Mersey Square though, for it is now culverted and actually goes underneath the modern shopping centre. Its modern stores are a far cry from a quaint old sweet shop which stood here once upon a time. The owner loved children and noticed how disappointed they were when they came in with a coin or two to spend and were only able to buy a couple of his creations. He knew that many had worked long hours to earn those coins and so decided to make miniature sweets for them. He gave the first ones to his daughter to try and she gave one to her dolly. As a result, despite all else that Stockport gave to this world, 'dolly mixture' is probably the most delightful.

It gave us much more and once had the largest Sunday school in the world, for children and adults to go on their one day off to learn how to read and write, besides something of the Bible stories. Associated with it was one of the most remarkable of Victorian families. One sister was the mother of Stanley Baldwin; the Prime Minister who told Edward VIII to choose between the Throne and the woman he loved. Another courted her husband by Rudyard Lake on the Staffordshire border and named her son after it as Rudyard Kipling, counted by many as the greatest writer of the British Empire. His books and poems of old India, especially *The Jungle Book*, are still popular. Two other sisters married great Victorian artists, one Sir Edwin Poynter noted for scenes of life in the ancient world, another Sir Edwin Burne Jones. All the sisters modelled for his paintings dressed as Bible figures or saints in the stained glass he designed for numerous churches. No 'frowzy frights' they!

We have much to thank Stockport for besides its industry, which is explained in a special museum of hatting and a heritage centre in the old church by the wonderful Victorian cast iron and glass market. Amongst the treasures at the old Vernon Park Museum is the famous Blue John Window made from polished sections of this attractive rock from Castleton in Derbyshire. There are other windows made from it as it can be polished like glass, but Stockport's is the biggest.

 ## STYAL

Styal was given to the National Trust because of its beautiful valley near to the station to which people could come from Manchester to enjoy the countryside. It is still tree lined and amongst them is a giant redwood and rare rhododendrons, as plant collecting was a family passion. Now it is one of the most popular attractions in the area as people come to learn about the early cotton industry and hear about the lives of children from workhouses. The Apprentice House where they all lived is now open and restored to give an idea of what it might have been like. The garden could easily be overlooked, but it is one of few places where old varieties of garden plants are cultivated as they may well have special qualities which could make their seeds valuable in the future.

Samuel Greg, who built the mill in 1784, is credited with being a good employer by the standards of his day, but was he? Two boys ran away to London, and were questioned by the magistrates. Their testimony - that they were well treated, the mill was whitewashed once a year and they had reasonable food - has been taken as proof that Greg was in advance of his time. In fact the magistrate questioned them word for word from the printed Factory Act and that is exactly what the clerk wrote down. They simply said yes to each question. Greg was doing exactly what the law demanded and no more. Even the truth of this must be doubted, for when asked if they were given lessons in reading and writing they said that they were, but neither boy could even write his own name and signed with a cross.

A more disturbing story relates to Esther Price, whose indenture from Liverpool workhouse records she 'looked about 9 years old' when she was sent to work here. She was no orphan and we can only guess why she was parted from her mother who sent her a few shillings. This tempted her to want to go home, but when she was captured and returned the usual punishment was to cut off all her hair. With short hair in fashion the impact of this is lost on modern generations. No girls had short hair then and she would be marked out for years as a figure of fun and abuse. The French punished women who had been too friendly with the Germans during the War in the same way. Her eventual punishment was hardly better, she was locked in the dark in the attic at the Apprentice House, until the old woman who looked after it died and there was nowhere else to put the coffin with her inside. Both were left together in the dark until local protests assured Esther was released.

Later in the mill's history a school and other facilities including adult education classes were provided and conditions improved but this was after the apprentice system ended. Then whole families of labourers who had had to rely on the poor law to provide for them were sent to Styal as an alternative to going into the workhouse. Their rows of cottages each had a cellar which was planned to hold a hand loom so that the father could stay at home hand weaving while his family worked at spinning in the mill. However, the introduction of power looms resulted in the use of the cellars as dwellings for young couples until they started to have families, or older couples whose children had all grown up. The little village shop is preserved with examples of old fashioned packages in the window, but look out for a board hanging next to it. This was the communal 'laying out board'. When anyone died someone would go along to collect it to prepare the body for the funeral as it would take time for an undertaker to come from Wilmslow.

There is a little riddle about the clock that I used to ask students when I was an Education Officer there. The records show that Greg employed seven clockmakers - but he only had one clock - why? It was because in his day there were no mechanics, so it was people who had been apprenticed to clockmakers who made the works for his machines. The walls which line the road down to the mill have their own little tale. During the 'cotton famine', when British firms refused to handle cotton picked by slaves during the American Civil War the family used their men to build them. Though there was no work in the mill they could earn something and not be tempted to move away.

Another face of Styal is the well known women's prison. Its buildings can be seen from the road and have a story which links to the children in the mill. By the end of the 19th century concerns for children whose parents were not married, or simply could not afford to keep them, had changed from the days of workhouses. The city of Manchester designed their Cottage Homes in 1898 and they do look like a charming village surrounded by a high fence. Each was made to be as like a family community as possible and an older boy and girl were appointed 'parents' to help look after the younger ones. There were 600 children in 28 houses, taught in their own school, while every effort to find them good jobs was made when they were old enough. Yet it was far enough from the city to prevent ideas of running away. When family planning reduced the number of unwanted children to such an extent that finding enough children for the people who wanted to adopt one was a problem, the buildings were converted to the present use. It is interesting to find two completely different attitudes to children in the same village. While many come to find out about the Apprentice House few know of the Cottage Homes.

SUTTON LANE ENDS

A village nestling in the hills not far from Macclesfield has memories of three famous men in its old gritstone cottages. Raphael Holinshed was born here and wrote the famous *Chronicles* on which Shakespeare is known to have based his history plays. In the forge the young James Brindley (born 1716) was sent to serve as apprentice. His master despaired that he would ever make a living when he managed to build a wheel 'back to front' but he was not the illiterate man some make out. He was possibly dyslexic and had problems putting his ideas on paper. It was Brindley who built the Bridgewater Canal and started the Transport Revolution. The forge no longer functions but there is a plaque set in the wall, while another is set into the wall of a barn adjoining the cottage where the artist Charles Tunnicliffe grew up in the early 1900s. He is best remembered for pictures of birds, some of which are exhibited in Macclesfield Museum. The Gritstone Trail passes nearby and there is an unusual stone with a cross formed by cutting away part of the surface. It deserves entry here for the fact that different books give different stories. One that it is Saxon, others that it marks the burial of plague victims, is a boundary mark and even an attempt to make a pagan standing stone Christian. It is there for you to consider the options.

 ## SWETTENHAM

By virtue of a long lane and a deep ford to get to it, Swettenham must be included, but the huge car park at the pub hardly marks it out as hidden. You are advised to take the bridge; many years ago I tried to cross the ford on a bike but got stuck in the middle! Its church is a mixture of 18th century brickwork and Victorian stone pretending to be Norman. Above one door there is a cast lead donkey's head, the crest of the Mainwarings which is found also at Acton and Over Peover. There is what is claimed to be a Saxon cross but it is unlike others in the county and lacks decoration. Some claim the origin of the name was an early church dedicated to St Swithun - he of the 40 days of rain fame. Most people choose to seek it out in spring when Daffodil Dell with its 17th century timber-framed, water-powered saw mill, which is still operated, attracts people to the Dane Valley. Every year more daffodil bulbs are added by the family who have worked the mill for generations and their visitors. 'The Quinta' is the home of Sir Bernard Lovell who was in charge of building Jodrell Bank; the gardens are sometimes open to the public in summer.

TABLEY

Close to the M6, stands stately Tabley Hall, designed by John Carr of York in 1761. Colonel John Leicester Warren, a bachelor, wanted the National Trust to take over when he died.

They were unable to, but Manchester University stepped in and purchased the estate as an investment, which provided an opening for a new use for the larger part of the building as a complex of homes for the retired and facilities for their visitors. It is therefore still a lived in house.

Sir John Leicester was a collector of contemporary art at the start of the 19th century and built up a magnificent collection in his London home. He wanted the nation to use it as the foundation of a National Collection of British Art. Then, more involved with the aftermath of the Napoleonic wars and fears of revolution and rebellion, the Government declined. Most of the collection came back to Tabley. It provides a rare chance to see a collection representing the taste of a specific period.

One unique collection would be more than enough for most villages, but Tabley has two. By the main road the village school has taken on a new life as the home of the only Cuckoo Clock Museum in the world. The collection contains many fine examples and it is well worth making sure you are there when they all call out the hour, as they are all working.

The Windmill pub near the Tabley junction on the M6 used to have a sign with a scene from the novel *Don Quixote*, showing him, lance in hand, riding at a windmill which he believed was a giant. That along with the original sign for the Smoker pub at Plumley were painted by a Miss Leighton, a niece of Lord de Tabley. It has been replaced with a sign showing a racehorse. Someone got their stories or pubs mixed; for if Windmill was a de Tabley horse, surely Miss Leighton would have shown it as one as she did at the Smoker.

 # TARPORLEY

It is a comfortable village with a wide street lined with Georgian buildings, many now converted to shops, old inns and especially the Swan Hotel. This has a room upstairs which is the inner sanctum, the 'holy of holies' of the Hunt Club. Actually chasing foxes was less important than attending for a meal in the correct dress, right down to the sewing on the buttonholes or the right pockets. Arthur Barry of Marbury was fined one guinea for incorrect attire in 1768. The costume was colourful to say the least, and when Sir William Beechey was commissioned to paint the President, Sir Peter Warburton, in his official uniform he commented that he might as well have been asked to paint a parrot!

The parish church contains splendid and well known 18th and 19th century monuments to the Done family showing a variety of styles. John Done is shown with the famous hunting horn of Delamere Forest, which is now in the Grosvenor Museum in Chester. Two sisters in 17th century fashions are of interest for Mary Crewe, who was alive when the sculpture was made, is portrayed resting on one arm with an open book and open eyes. Her sister Jane Done was dead and is shown asleep with her book, representing her life, firmly closed. Mary's son John is depicted in the style of a generation later with a periwig looking incongruous when worn with a toga! Marble cherubs cry marble tears for him.

 ## TARVIN

This is a pretty place with streets cut from the living rock and timber-framed cottages rubbing shoulders with Georgian houses. The name has its origins in the Celtic word for a boundary, which could indicate that in Roman times the River Gowy marked a sort of boundary between the lands set aside for the legion in Chester. Its church has things for seekers of the unusual. There is a squint - an opening which allowed people in a side chapel to see the altar. If you look back through it from the altar you will see 'The Tarvin Imp'. Not so famous as the Lincoln one, but also supporting the roof.

Look also for the brass epitaph of Henry Hardware, one time Mayor of Chester. The hole in it was caused by a musket ball when Royalist and Roundhead fought around the church. Hardware was responsible for digging up the Bull Ring in Chester to prevent bull baiting and for ending the summer parade which included giants, the devil and 'naked boys'. Tarvin was a centre of Puritanical beliefs. John Bruen smashed the ancient stained glass from the windows in his chapel and had it replaced with clear glass as he objected to the pictures of saints which he considered no better than idols. Cast an eye on the gravestone in the church tower of John Thomasen with a quill pen. He was said to do calligraphy better than anyone else of his day and copied poems for Queen Anne, but also taught in the village school here.

TATTON PARK

This needs no introduction as one of the National Trust's biggest attractions, but in the park it is worth seeking out the old hall. It gives an experience of medieval living, with a central fire in the great hall which is covered by the curfew at the end of the session. Other rooms were reconstructed from a 17th century inventory and as original furnishings were unobtainable exact copies of items in museums were made. Around the hall are humps and hollows in the fields, remnants of the old village whose inhabitants were moved to Rostherne to improve the view. Information boards explain what you see while an introduction to old time farming is housed in a timber-framed barn which was falling into disrepair in Frodsham and was rebuilt here. When the park was laid out there were plans for two lakes, but only one was created to save money. Eventually a second mere was formed when the ground sank into salt springs exactly where intended. Lord Egerton christened it Melchet Mere after Lord Melchet, the chairman of ICI.

THELWALL

Travellers today know the name because of a huge viaduct which crosses both the Mersey and the Ship Canal carrying the M6. The seeker for the curious will look virtually underneath it for reminders of Saxon times and the Danish invasions. The Pickering Arms is not nearly so old but has an inscription taken from the *Anglo Saxon Chronicle* which records the date AD 923 (in Roman numerals) and that 'In this year went King Edward with a force after harvest to Thelwall and bade build the City and occupy it and man it'. Of course that did not mean a city with a cathedral nor any great population as we understand the term today, it was a citadel or fortified place. It was one of a number of places which were fortified at this time of the Danish invasions into Cheshire to protect the northern parts of Mercia.

THORNTON HOUGH

Cheshire is rich in fantasy estate villages. One of the many such jewels in Cheshire's crown is Thornton Hough which owes its form to an Anglican and a Unitarian who both gave excellent churches to the village. All Saints is unusual because it has five clocks on the tower. When it was built Joseph Hirst, a textile manufacturer who originally came from Yorkshire, found he could not see the clock from his house so had the extra face added higher up. He died in 1874. Then came William Lever of Port Sunlight fame, with all his entourage of architects to give the village a complete 'make over'. In Port Sunlight he made an industrial town look beautiful. Here he made his ideal of an English country village, constructing a Unitarian chapel which looks more like a parish church with a splendid lych gate. Sumptuous timber-framed houses, a village green with a thatched shelter and a lot more to delight the eye. He made his fortune from the Victorian obsession with health and cleanliness and was passionate about fresh air; his bedroom had no glass in the windows. This resulted in a chill that turned to pneumonia and killed him. On special days you can visit the grounds and see the wonderful gardens.

Near to it are a series of avenues which were laid out for Leverhulme just before the First World War. They have a central road and footpaths separated from it by rows of trees. It is believed to have been the start of a scheme to build a whole new town in the Wirral which was cut short by the war and the following depression.

 ## THREE SHIRES BRIDGE

In a remote situation where Cheshire, Derbyshire and Staffordshire borders meet is an old stone bridge, seldom visited except by ramblers in the hills. Its position made it a favourite meeting place for those with less than legal intents in the past, including the Flash gang of illicit coin makers and barefist fighters. Should a Cheshire constable arrive they would simply jump into another shire, where he could not follow them; if two constables arrived they would go into the third county. The chances of three constables all arriving at the same time and cutting off their escape were so remote that they were hardly hampered in their illicit dealings.

 # THURSTATON

You will find Thor's Stone, a natural outcrop, in the middle of the common and nearby is Thingwall where the parliament of the Norse settlers of these parts met (the Tinwald is still the Parliament of the Isle of Man and the oldest parliament in the world). They did not just raid and pillage, those Norse of old, but settled and set up farming and trading communities. Archaeology has repainted the traditional image created by Saxon priests who feared the fierce pagans. They had settled in Ireland with a capital at Dublin which was very civilised for its day, and also on the Isle of Man. They were allowed to settle in the Wirral as a foothold for their trading activities in the Irish Sea on condition that they remained there and did not attack the rest of the county. Places names ending in 'by' were founded by them. It is part of the Wirral Country Park and an information centre has been provided by the County Council. J. Pearson, designer of Truro Cathedral, was responsible for the church in 1885, though he left the tower of the older church standing in the churchyard. Some items from the earlier church have been saved including the old font and the shelves on which charity bread was put for the poor.

 # TIRLEY GARTH

A grand house, which opens its gardens to the public from time to time especially when the rhododendrons are in bloom. It was started in 1909 for Bryan Leesmith, a Director of Brunner Mond, but he left the company before it was finished and the house passed to them. The company leased it to R.H. Prestwich, whose family produced the Burberry raincoats. During the Second World War Irene Prestwich used it for the work of the 'Oxford Group' who became known as 'Moral Rearmament'. They were and are a non denominational group aimed at establishing traditional values of honesty, unselfishness and love, encouraging discussion of problems rather than violence and following the teachings of Frank Buchman. The house was purchased after the war with funds she raised and is now used as the organisation's conference centre which can accommodate up to 120 guests at any one time.

The house was built in Arts and Crafts style by C. F. Mallows, a student of Lutyens, but with much in common with the work of Norman Shaw. It comes as something of a surprise to see so hard and 'modern' a house in Cheshire, better known for half timber and red sandstone. It has large windows and extensive walls covered with pebble dash - a new and exciting material at that time with none of the modern overtones of covering up poor workmanship.

TUSHINGHAM

Look out for the old Bell o'the Hill, which is in a side lane since the Whitchurch road took a new route behind it. This quaint half-timbered hostelry has a tale to tell. A duck once hatched from an egg on the hearth under the ancient chimney and was to have been the children's pet. It became a bossy bird pecking everyone who came near and so it was decided to make Sunday dinner of it. The children refused to eat their pet, which was buried, but then a ghost of a duck continued to peck everyone. A real bad tempered duck was bad enough for trade, but a spooky one . . . ! Seven parsons assembled and charmed it until it was small enough to be put into a bottle and hidden in the

The Bell o' the Hill, Tushingham

cellar walls. According to traditions glass had magic properties and spirits could be imprisoned in bottles. When alterations were made between the wars the bottle was lifted out, and carefully replaced.

Ask for directions at the Bell to the old church of St Chad, standing almost forgotten in the fields. It is still furnished in the 18th century style as a new church replaced it and saved it from devastating restorations. In the churchyard is a rare curio, the hearse house still has its horse-drawn glass-sided Victorian vehicle looking like a prop from a horror film. One might find oneself looking at the map twice in this district as 'The Land of Canaan' is clearly shown. It was given that name by a farmer to represent his 'promised land'. Another name echoing the religious fervour of the 19th century is above the door of the little Methodist chapel on Bradley Common which proudly states that it is 'Poor Man's Bethel'.

 ## UPTON

Upton is best known for Chester Zoo, one of the world's foremost centres for breeding endangered animals. It was one of the first to get rid of the bars of cages and actually recycled a lot of concrete which had been used as road blocks in case of German invasion during the Second World War to create things for the animals to climb over; an aspect of conservation not usually considered.

In the churchyard is the plague stone; at times of infection it was filled with vinegar and anyone who might carry disease could put their coins into it. Then after a time traders would come and take the coins and leave food by its side, in an attempt to prevent cross infection long before anyone really understood how diseases spread. It once stood at the crossroads but was moved here for safety. A similar stone can be seen in Warrington Museum.

 ## UTKINTON

The old hall is much too big for modern living and parts look in need of care and attention. It has memories of long ago.

The Dones became High Foresters of Delamere and in the Middle Ages provided oak trees for the restoration of the salt well in Middlewich and the bridge at Northwich from the forest, for which they received saplings to replace the forest stock. Their duty was to accompany the Earl of Chester, who was also Prince of Wales, or the monarch when they visited the forest and the ancient horn which was their badge of office is now proudly displayed in the Grosvenor Museum in Chester. The last monarch to hunt there was James I who knighted John Done, heir of the Dones, after successfully killing a stag. You can see his image holding the famous horn in Tarporley church. Charles I ordered that all the deer should be killed as he had no intention of hunting so far from London. Later, the forest was enclosed. Now the great house is the centre of a farm in a country lane.

VALE ROYAL

One of the finest of golf courses covers the remains of the abbey church. A few stones assembled from the ruins are wrongly known as the Nun's Grave, but despite two fanciful novels the term probably originated as Nuns' Grove. Someone could not read old handwriting! It was a wood belonging to the nuns of Chester in which the abbey was built, as mentioned in the abbey ledger. Old writing is notoriously difficult to understand and someone let imagination take over from logic. Although the stones now stand fairly close to the site of the old high altar, an engraving in Ormerod's history of Cheshire shows they were first set up as a focus opposite the front door of the house. The genuine enough decorated top was found in 1813 and has a 14th century carving of St Nicholas, who besides being associated with Christmas is also the patron saint of shipwrecked sailors. Prince Edward, then Earl of Chester and later Edward I, was crossing the sea when a mighty storm threatened to drown him. He vowed if he was saved he would build the fairest and finest Cistercian abbey in England. He came to Vale Royal in 1277 to lay the foundation stone and the same year he set off on invading Wales. It was a grand gesture at the start of the invasion, followed by the biggest building project undertaken by any medieval monarch in Europe, when linked with constructing the Welsh castles and rebuilding the walls at Chester. Then a major fire required a rebuilding in Chester, which is believed to have been the origin of the famous rows. It almost bankrupted the country. He could not repay loans to Italian bankers and took Walter de Hereford the master mason away from Vale Royal to complete Caernarvon Castle, leaving the monks to struggle for the next 60 years to complete their church only to see it, ironically enough, destroyed by a storm.

Later it was the country house of the Cholmondeleys who became Lords Delamere. In the house there is said to be a secret room which the heir was shown on his 21st birthday; he would never tell what he had seen. No trace was found during recent extensive restorations. One secret that was revealed was that the King's Room, which was said to have been prepared for a visit by James I in 1617 could not have been, for the back of the panels had marks left by circular saws.

The foundations of the abbey lie hidden under the lawns but to find other treasures you must go far afield. Finds from the excavation are stored at the Grosvenor Museum, Chester. One of the best known pictures in the Tate Gallery is the *Cholmondeley Sisters* which shows them in bed with new born babies. No one is exactly sure who they were but according to the label they were born on the same day and had their child on the same day and are shown in bed in full Elizabethan court dress. Until the estates were sold by Lord Delamere, who had settled in Kenya and pioneered white settlements in the cooler highlands, it had hung in Vale Royal. The stained glass went from the sale to the Burrel Collection in Glasgow and is displayed in the windows of their restaurant. The glass panels which show the Prince's vow to found the abbey and what is presumed to represent his permission to move from Darnhall to Vale Royal also went there. The style makes art historians conclude that they were copied from the initial letters of destroyed charters drawn up in the Royal Court in London authorising the two events.

The final long distance travellers are a chalice and paten which were found at Dolgellau in Wales. It has been suggested, but not proved, that they were made for Vale Royal. Edward is known to have collected all the seals of the Welsh princes and melted them down to make a chalice for Vale Royal, so they could not be used again. The paten has the inscription 'Walter made me out of Hereford'. Walter of Hereford was the second Abbot and moved from Dore Abbey in Herfordshire, but it was also the name of the mason in charge of the building. One or the other may have given a matching piece. How they got to Wales is a mystery. What is more ironic is that if it really was the chalice made from the seals of Welsh chieftains to show their suppression, it is now one of the greatest treasures of the National Museum of Wales in Cardiff, an appropriate twist of fate.

WALLASEY

It gained its name from the Saxon word for a native from which we get the name Wales; this was the 'walla's isle'. It still has miles of sandy beaches and a tunnel to Liverpool. Wallasey lost its most interesting old building in 1965 because the chairman of the Planning Committee preferred to see a block of flats set up on the site. Mother Redcap's had been a centre for smuggling, and an old inn. A new owner wanted to bring it up to date as a social club but the Council refused to give it a licence and it was demolished. It once had a dummy weather vane - if it pointed to the house it was clear for smugglers and others, if it pointed away it warned them to stay away. Wirral was notorious for smuggling and wreckers who would set false signals to lure ships into dangerous places. Then it became a fashionable place for those whose trade came from Liverpool's docks to settle away from the bustle and by the sea.

Once known for races, Mockbeggar Hall at Leasowe originated in the 16th century as a tower from which Ferdinando, Earl of Derby, and his guests could watch them, but it also provided ample accommodation for them to stay for a time. Later it became a convalescent home for injured railwaymen to recuperate by the sea.

WALTON

A pretty model estate village of the Victorian period built for Sir Gilbert Greenall, Baronet, one of the brewing family from Warrington. The hall was being built when Queen Victoria came to the throne and is an impressive building. Near it is the church of 1885, only one of many that Sir Gilbert built between Warrington and Northwich. Great Budworth had the second highest number of townships in the country to serve. Greenall helped provide most of them with their own village churches, many of which became parishes in their own right. The Warrington Crematorium is in this pleasant setting, which must have been much more appreciated in the days when Warrington was a smoky industrial town. Now the hall and the park are administered by Warrington Borough Council as a pleasant amenity. Refreshments are available in the hall where there are also exhibition facilities and there is a children's zoo. The busy main road has been diverted to leave the pretty houses undisturbed.

WARBURTON

The old church was abandoned in favour of a new one and fortunately this has involved the preservation of its historic interior filled with box pews and old woodwork of yesteryear. It has been the subject of archaeological investigations. You have to get special permission to see inside, but one secret can be seen from the churchyard. It is a confusing building as the tower is at the 'wrong' end, but look for the vestry door at the bottom of it and you will see a small peep hole at eye level. Tradition has it that this was where members of a family who had recently buried someone in the churchyard could stay for a few nights afterwards. They could look out if there was any sign of disturbance and prevent body snatchers. There is a large scale model of the church in the Local History Library in Sale if you have trouble seeing inside. Near the church are the steps of an old wayside cross and the stocks with shackles for a whipping post.

WARMINGHAM

They say 'proud Warmingham poor people, new church old steeple' as the 18th century tower was left when the rest was rebuilt a century later. In the churchyard, by the wall behind the altar you will find a broken gravestone. It once represented a skeleton resting in the grave, and was a typical 18th century way of showing the resurrection. Some person with little understanding or sense has smashed it. Part of the medieval churchyard cross has been converted to a sundial and close by, a weir provided water for the old mill which is now used for industrial workshops.

WARRINGTON

On entering the library and museum you might miss a stone plaque which proclaims that it was the first library supported out of the rates. There is a tale of the grim days after the Peterloo Massacre when the Government taxed books and periodicals and would only allow local authorities to finance a library if it was in a museum and referred to the collection. Printed propaganda had been instrumental in starting the French Revolution and they were worried about its effects here. Warrington was one of only four museums with a library which operated under that Act. To satisfy the town's 'thirst for knowledge' it was originally housed in the Black Boy pub near the church. Then in 1848 the Government allowed authorities to finance public libraries as long as two thirds of voters agreed. As it already had one, Warrington became the first authority to finance its public library.

As one of the oldest municipal museums in Britain it is fitting that it is 'the sort of museum that belongs in a museum'. A delightful peep at Victorian times when museums tried to act as a local encyclopaedia of knowledge, and here all set out and classified as the Victorians loved to do, are fossils, animals, birds, insects and plants. There are Roman, prehistoric and medieval remains or curiosities of many kinds and every one worthy of attention. Long may it remain so! It would be a tragedy if someone decided to get rid of all this and replace it with the 'book on a wall' sort of display that too many museums have adopted.

The church contains an unusual legacy, the chapel of the South Lancashire Regiment, who were garrisoned in the town when it was still part of Lancashire. It has their banners, with a sphinx a reminder of their days in Egypt in Napoleonic times, and Warrington has its Cairo Street as a reminder. The church is the only one dedicated to St Elphin. No one knows who he or she was. There is a St Elphin's Well and it may be that it was a local pagan god, disguised as a saint by early Christians or an early preacher long forgotten.

Holy Tinity church tower near the centre has a few things to catch the eye. First of all it is built over a right of way (as are Sandbach and St Michael's in Chester) but the interest is in the clock which is a separate structure sitting on the church tower. In the early days of the factories many unscrupulous owners had special clocks made which would add an extra hour of unpaid work each day to the time worked. In order to combat this the Government passed a Factory Act to say that every town had to have a public clock for the workers to check their time against. St Elphin's was far away from the town centre so a publicly owned clock was set up on Holy Trinity church tower. It is still the property and responsibility of the Borough and not the church.

Near the bridge over the Mersey you can still find the old Academy with the statue of Oliver Cromwell made by the Ironbridge Company in 1862. They also made gates which were intended for Sandringham, but when Queen Victoria saw Oliver Cromwell exhibited next to them in London she decided against the offer. After rusting for a time back at Ironbridge they were purchased for Warrington Town Hall. The Academy was one of several which were built in the days when Oxford and Cambridge would not admit Nonconformists, but they were the leading lights of the Industrial Revolution. Amongst the scholars who are associated with Warrington Academy was Joseph Priestley who discovered oxygen - the joke is that he didn't find it until after he left Warrington! He also gave us fizzy drinks. Another strange shadowy character was a Msr Marat who taught French, who some believe was the same Marat who organised the 'Terror' after the French Revolution arguing that all aristocrats should die. He himself met an untimely death, killed by Charlotte Corday, in his bath as painted by David.

In the 1980s a revolution of a sort started here. Eddie Shah took over the *Warrington Guardian* series of newspapers, and hired the Acadamy for his offices. He was the first to introduce modern computer technology to newspaper printing and publishing in general. Eventually this was to see the closure of the old printing works in Fleet Street and riots outside his works at Wapping, but now all printing is done the way which started here. Something that none of the old scholars could have believed was that when a new and improved roadway to the bridge was needed they actually put the whole Academy - and Cromwell as well - onto rollers and moved them out of the way.

WEAVERHAM

An old village centre is surrounded by housing estates built for workers at ICI during the 1950s. The thatched Poplar Cottage functioned until recently as the village carpenter's shop, but his workshop has now been converted into a bungalow. He made the coffins for the dead who were 'laid out' in the workshop. A door at one side gave access to a special chamber where there was a bed which acted as maternity ward for the village. It was tradition that if you were born downstairs and carried up you would rise in life, but be born upstairs and there was no hope! A woman would lie in the chamber until her 'churching'. It has now been joined to the rest of the house. A room at the Wheatsheaf pub was known as 'Parliament' or 'Knowledge Room' because folk met there to discuss the events of the day though it may have originated as simply a parlour.

At Hefferstone Grange new houses surround the fine 18th century house. Careless development saw the best baroque plaster ceiling in Cheshire destroyed in 1998. It dated from 1741 and showed Julius Caesar, Augustus and Homer, but when I sent someone to photograph it they found it in bits in a skip waiting to go to the tip. There is a tale still told of Robina, daughter of Mr Heath, a Liverpool slave trader turned country gentleman who wanted his daughter to marry a man with a title. Instead she eloped with the garden boy, both riding bicycles - probably only as far as the nearest station. When she returned she was disowned and they went to live in a small cottage.

Weaverham Gate takes its name from the old word for a main road and the inn of that name still has a stone mounting block outside its old stables, now converted to extra hospitality space. John Wesley records spending a night at Weaverham Gate, but we are not sure if that was at the hostelry or just in the district. Like others at Winsford and Sutton it had a gate hanging with the rhyme:

This gate hangs high and hinders none,
Refresh, pay and journey on.

West Kirby

It is believed to have had one of the earliest churches in the county dedicated to St Bridget, which could indicate that followers of the Celtic Church settled here in pagan days. She was, however, a popular saint in the Celtic world and it is well known that Christian Norse from Ireland settled the Wirral and they may have dedicated the church to an Irish saint in memory of their homeland. Although little of the church is ancient it retains a few antiquities to remind us of the Norse including fragments of Nordic crosses and a hog's back gravestone of a Nordic chieftain. Amongst the saints on the outside of the church you will find evidence of the date of the present building in carvings depicting Queen Victoria, the Prince of Wales (later Edward VII), Gladstone and Disraeli.

Somewhere near here a girl was drowned bringing the cattle home when the tide changed, and the story gave us a well known poem:

> The western tide crept up along the sand,
> As far as the eye could see,
> The rolling mist came down and hid the land,
> And never home came she,
> But still the boatmen hear her call the cattle home,
> Across the sands of Dee.

It was written by Charles Kingsley, a canon of Chester Cathedral who knew these shores well. He loved nature and would lead parties from the city into the wilds of Wales or Cheshire to explore the natural history. Many came, rich and poor, educated and simple. Few could relate to the countryside like he could and he published many learned articles for the Chester Natural History Society. The Natural History room at the Grosvenor Museum is dedicated to his memory. He is best known for changing a cruel aspect of the law. According to the story one day a little boy came down his chimney, having taken a wrong route. He told the kindly man of the sufferings of the little boys - the smaller the better - who were sent up chimneys to sweep them. The result was a wonderful story, *The Water Babies*, which linked his love of nature and his worries for the poor of the towns. It raised public outrage and the use of little boys to clean chimneys was banned.

WESTON

There are four villages in the Runcorn district, Norton, Aston (east-ton), Sutton and Weston, which show there were farms here in Saxon times and in the centre of them is Cheshire's own Stockholm; a place which was originally defended by a stockade. Weston has been much in the news recently because of an abandoned quarry. At one time it was very important and was Runcorn's own 'Rock of The Dinosaurs', for large numbers of fossilised footprints were found in the sandstone during the 19th century. One of the biggest pieces is in the Manchester Museum where several huge slabs are fitted together and show countless tracks where small Triassic creatures, especially rhynchosaurs, ran over the wet mud. The reconstruction of what they looked like, made for Liverpool Museum, reminds me of beavers with two protruding teeth, they are about the same size but, of course, have no fur and lived around 200,000 years ago. As the mud cracked it formed a pattern like crazy paving and this can still be seen. The quarries at Weston and others at Storeton in the Wirral have produced more dinosaur tracks than any others in England so that Manchester and Liverpool Museums house the largest collections of fossil footprints in the country.

The stone was so good that it was used to build the Anglican cathedral at Liverpool, and the altar is of fine grained stone from Weston with gold leaf to cover parts of it. It was used to repair Chester Cathedral, as the stone was less likely to be weather damaged, and for the columns at Tatton and Tabley Halls. It was mainly used by the Weaver Navigation for their locks and other buildings and proved to be so good it was even exported to New York for use in the docks there! During the early 20th century there was no longer a market for good stone as concrete became the normal building material. The quarries were abandoned and deserted.

The nearby chemical works needed a place to tip their waste material and, with little regard to conservation, the historic importance of the quarries and future pollution, tons of waste were used to fill the quarry and level the ground. In the year 2000 this had disastrous results as the gases produced by the chemicals percolated through the sandstone and into the nearby houses. Many of them have been abandoned altogether. Few places have its advantages of a wide view over the Mersey and seen from this distance even the chemical works in Runcorn and Widnes have a certain visual attraction, especially at night when they show countless lights reflected in the Mersey. In the distance the two great cathedrals of the Liverpool skyline can be seen at night too when floodlights illuminate one and the lights inside the central stained glass lantern show the other one. It is a unique viewpoint made all the more poignant by the fact that the stone for the huge emblem of faith on the horizon came from almost under your feet.

WETTENHALL

Old folks jokingly say any small man is 'like the Little Man o' Wettna' and his pub has an image of him over the door. He was Billy Grice of Chester who made wooden meat skewers in the winter and wandered the country lanes to sell them in the summer. There is also *Wettna Long Lane* which seems longer because it is so flat and has no turnings. Peewits are said to fly 'backards' along it, but I've yet to see it. Actually, it is used to say that something is unlikely - rather like 'pigs might fly'. With some of the things listed in this book you might exclaim the same.

WHITEGATE

A pretty thatched cottage and an old white house look over the green. The house was a pub until Lady Delamere objected to people drinking after church and had it converted into a house. The cottage deserves a second look for in the housing shortage of the 18th and 19th centuries such cottages were often split into two or three one-room dwellings with a little sleeping space in the loft. This has remained separate, though as times change each 'dwelling' has a huge extension to the back making two modern homes tacked onto an old frontage on the village green. In the church the arms of Charles II are interesting as they actually portray the old crown destroyed by Cromwell as the new crown was not made in 1660 when it was painted.

In the churchyard rests Sir David Muirhead Bone, the first war artist employed by the Government, next to his son who was a promising scholar who contracted tuberculosis. The exclusive Mundsley Sanatorium, where he was a patient, was moved from Norfolk to Vale Royal for safety during the Second World War and his parents chose to be buried next to him in this quiet and peaceful spot. A little way along the road is the Monkey Lodge, a strange little building covered with baroque carvings which have evidently been reused from a grander building. It might look as if someone has 'monkeyed around' with the architecture, but its name is older; it was the monks' lodge by a drive over the fields.

WIDNES

The name is said to derive from a wide nose - nothing to do with the inhabitants, but the piece of land which pushes into the Mersey here. When the tide was out they used to be able to walk cattle over the sands to Runcorn, but when it was in sailing boats rushed on a three-way journey taking coal from the Sankey Brook Canal into the Weaver for mid Cheshire's salt-works, returning with salt for Liverpool and then taking cotton bales to the mills of Lancashire. It was once one of the most heavily polluted towns in England because of its chemical works and if you fell into the Mersey you were taken for immediate hospital treatment. Yet Widnes has a promenade and beach!

They seem as unlikely as Wigan Pier, but are far grander, allowing people to walk along the riverside and even to bathe in the waters which are usually salty when the tide is in. The name Snig (eel) Pie Island is a reminder of days when the Mersey was less polluted. An interesting feature of the Promenade is an outdoor pulpit in the walls of the churchyard. When built, nothing that resembled fun was allowed on the Sabbath. Children were not allowed to play with toys and hearing a sermon or reading from the Bible was the only acceptable 'entertainment'. In those days a walk along Widnes Prom was an excursion and a chance to show off in your best clothes, long before the days of package holidays in the sun.

Today the chemical industry has changed and parts of the river front are, unbelievably, developed for wildlife conservation. This does not extend to the flocks of starlings who spend the winter nights on the bridge, every effort to move them has failed. It is worth looking out for them at dusk just to see the aerial acrobatics as they swarm to rest on every available perch. In 1999 the Mersey was named as 'the most improved river in the world' so its prom and sands may come into their own again.

Music lovers will find Widnes Station and the plaque which recalls that while waiting for a train there Paul Simon wrote the words of his ever popular and haunting 'Homeward bound, I wish I was' - an understandable sentiment in old Widnes! Yes, this was the very railway station where he was sitting with a ticket for his destination after appearing at a local hall and missing his train 'on a tour of one night stands, suitcase and guitar in hands'.

 ## WILDBOARCLOUGH

The brook runs briskly through a valley in the hills, especially after heavy rain or melting snows. It is claimed the last wolf in England was killed nearby. In its valley, in the 18th century, young James Brindley went to see a water-driven paper mill with his master, who really had not much of an idea what to do. Brindley walked into Manchester to inspect similar ones and was so successful with the new technology that his wheel operated until 1952; when no one even considered trying to preserve it. It was the start of a career which culminated in the canal era. The mill changed to weaving carpets using Brindley's wheel and the pretty Edinburgh Cottages were built for Scottish weavers who were employed to teach local people how to operate the machines. There is a little row of them with gothic pointed windows by the roadside. There is a pretty little bridge with a plaque to remind us that on 24th May 1989 heavy rain made the valley flood causing much damage. At the northern end is the well known Cat and Fiddle, England's second highest pub, while the Stanley Arms in an intriguingly named valley, 'Bottom of the Oven', is overlooked by Shuttlings Low, one of the few true peaks in the part of the county which is in the Peak District National Park.

Stanley was the family name of Lord Derby who used Crag Hall when he wanted to get away from the troubles of the world. It was so far away that he missed an important meeting with Queen Victoria and had the old mill offices converted into the biggest sub-post office in England to receive telegraph messages. During the war, Winston Churchhill used Crag Hall because of this facility.

🌿 WILDERSPOOL

The Roman settlement of Veratinum is split by the Ship Canal and many finds were discovered when it was dug. The canal once formed the boundary between Lancashire and Cheshire and the Cheshire side was known as Stockton Heath to distinguish it. The largest excavations carried out on a Roman site in the North West took place here during the 1960s and 1970s, when huge areas were excavated to rescue every vestige of Roman remains before the sites were built over. They showed signs of various industries, including pottery and iron work carried out in huge timber buildings, one of which was 100 by 150 feet. It also showed an unusual mixture of native round houses and Roman rectangular ones. One should not regret that they were built upon, for once excavated there was not a thing left to preserve, as the buildings were only traced by stains in the sand where beams had rested.

Pottery made in kilns in Wilderspool has been found in the forts of Hadrian's Wall. It is more likely it was taken to Carlisle by boat than along the Roman road which was also a direct link with the Wall. Along with Northwich and Middlewich, Wilderspool formed part of what has been termed 'the Roman Black Country'. Many finds are on display in Warrington Museum and were discovered when extensions to the former brewery were made. The brewery used a classical maiden blowing a horn as their trade mark and it is said that the origin of the name was 'wild deer's pool'. Wild deer and the brewery have both long gone, but the name 'Long Causeway' survives to remind us of the days when the road to the old bridge over the Mersey had to be reached by a road raised on a bank above the river marshes.

WILLASTON

There are two: one near Crewe which is mainly residential, and the one which has the Wirral Way, a walk along an old railway line preserving access into the countryside, the first of its sort in Britain. One station remains at Hadlow Road, which has been preserved with old advertising signs etc to give an impression of village stations in the 1950s on the eve of Dr Beeching's cuts.

In the same road is the Wirral Stone. Actually there are three stones together like steps. Some claim it is a broken standing stone and marked an ancient land boundary, but no one really knows. Do not confuse it with the modern village sign which has a mill-stone set on a York stone base. (Why York in an area rich in native sandstone?) There have been attempts to show that the village took its name from the stone, but these have been discounted in the light of recent research which shows it was 'The Pissing Stone'. It was not obscene but an old way of saying posting - ie where official notices were posted. It was given its more acceptable name in Victorian times.

WILMSLOW

This was William's Low, or burial place, and the Bronze Age urn which possibly contained his ashes is in Manchester Museum. People would claim that there is no one living in Wilmslow as the church and churchyard is actually Wilmslow, but around it were ancient areas called Bollin Fee and Pownall Fee. Those names indicated that the people had undertaken to pay a set fee rather than fluctuating manorial taxes. In 1894 the new Urban District Council took the name of Wilmslow. The brass of Ralph and Douce del Booth is the oldest in the county and shows them holding hands, although they were only 7 and 9 when they married. For many years they lay in front of the altar, but when I took a party to see them they had been moved to a side chapel for protection. An interesting visual pun is in the effigy of Humphrey Newton whose head rests on three barrels - or tuns. It is a rebus (a visual pun) as his wife was a Sutton and his mother was a Fitton. Congleton used to use the same pun with two conga eels and a tun.

An early broadcaster on the countryside, a retired Methodist minister, the Rev G. Bramwell Evans is remembered here. Known to children in a pre-television era as 'Romany of the BBC' he used a traditional caravan for holidays and many believed he actually broadcast from it not from the studio in Manchester. His mother was a Romany and he captivated a generation with his vivid descriptions of the countryside. When he died in 1943 his caravan soon became a place of pilgrimage, especially as his dog 'Raq' lived on by it until 1947. Few now remember him, but he was a star in his day and his style set the pattern for nature broadcasting.

Pownall Hall on the Carrs (river banks) is an important house for art historians, built in 1886 for the brewer Henry Boddington using the best of Arts and Crafts designs. Next to it are the remains of a little chapel dedicated to St Olaf. It is not as old as you might think, but was created as the private chapel for the house using old stones. Only the foundations now remain. Near to it is an oak tree and a glacial boulder with an inscription telling an odd tale. When Lord Egerton cut the first sod of the Ship Canal at Eastham, Boddington, a Director, took it back home, planted an acorn in it and when it was established planted sod and oak next to the chapel. When he died his cremated ashes were scattered on the spot. Financial problems followed his death and the family moved away so the chapel was neglected and fell into ruins.

WINCHAM

A building in the New Cheshire Salt Works has a tale of a discovery which changed the way we live. During the Second World War developments on the idea of the jet engine were made. The initial experiments took place at Trafford Park, but when the building was hit by a bomb it was decided to look for a safer place. The manager came from the family which owned the salt works and offered to provide accommodation away from the risk of more bombs. A special building was set up with devices to test the engine's power in a version fixed into position. It was supposed to be top secret but the noises coming from the works set the whole district speculating on what was going on behind locked doors. A plaque still recalls the invention which eventually gave us holidays abroad and round the world travel.

WINCLE

It sounds as if it should be by the sea not in the rolling hills. Its pub, which is some way from the church in a lane lined with stone walls and tall hedges, also sounds nautical for it is the Ship Inn. Probably it had the same origin as the one in Styal where beer was first served in an old shippon (cow shed). It has a tale to tell; for the pub sign was given by Lady Brocklehurst of Swythamley, just over the Staffordshire border. It features the *Nimrod*, which was the explorer Shackleton's vessel, surrounded by ice with two figures and a sledge on the snow. Her son, Sir Peter, went with him on his expedition to the Antarctic in 1909. It was this ship that had to dock in a dreadful storm, but the ice on which they landed broke away so that part of the crew spent the night on an iceberg in the howling gale. The hundred mile an hour wind froze the sea as it blew over the ship and the team was eventually forced to turn back from the Pole. They were a well travelled family, the Brocklehursts, and their collection makes up the main part of the contents of Macclesfield Museum. They also maintained a small zoo and wallabies which escaped from there successfully colonised the moors around here. They like to keep hidden, but are occasionally spotted crossing the road. It is said that all British grey squirrels are also descended from a pair which the Brocklehursts released into their park.

High on the moors in a small wood is Cleulow Cross, one of the round shafted types which were set up under the Nordic invaders. Not far from it another round shaft belongs to the Post Office tower, a landmark to be seen for many miles.

WINNINGTON

Winnington has a strange claim to fame as polythene was discovered in the laboratories here and was made during the Second World War as an insulator for radar. Hitler claimed it gave the allies the advantage in the Battle of the Atlantic. After the war production was nearly abandoned as no one could find any use for it. Then in the 1950s it became the new wonder product from which everything from rainwear to scrubbing brushes was made. During the war the first secret attempts at producing an atomic bomb were also made here and in the First World War discoveries helped make this an area for explosives production; later the artificial fertilisers industry developed from advances made here. It was all part of the great chemical works of Brunner Mond which became one of the major parts of ICI in 1926, but reorganisation has seen the old name revived. It still produces soda ash, which is one of the most useful chemicals there is and is essential in a range of products from glass to soap making. It is slightly ironic that the ash has the same chemical formula as the natron which the Ancient Egyptians used to preserve their mummies and thousands of years later John Brunner gave some of the profits from making it to found the chair of Egyptology at Liverpool University. He paid towards the excavations at Abydos: the sanctuary of Orisis - the god of mummification!

Lost within the giant works is an easily overlooked gem. The Hall is partly Tudor and part the work of one of the Wyatts. After many years as a private club for managers, there is a restaurant here and the rooms can be hired for receptions etc. It has many tales. The Winnington Letters of John Ruskin have been published and tell of the great art historian's friendships with the girls of the school in the Hall when it was a pretty place in the Weaver valley. It was so attractive that two views of it were included on the great dinner service which Wedgwood made for Catherine the Great of Russia. Sir John Brunner and Ludwig Mond purchased the house and lived in separate sides while setting up the first factory in the former park in 1874. As Brunner married his housekeeper, Mrs Mond considered her nothing more than a servant even when she became Lady Brunner. They lived in the same house without ever speaking.

The 'Winnington Lady' supposedly died when she tried to slit a vein in her wrist to stop herself blushing when a certain young man arrived at a ball. Instead she cut an artery and fell down the great stairs to die at his feet where the story says the bloodstains can still be seen. I told this tale at an old folks' home and a voice from the back chimed up, 'I scrubbed them steps for 40 years and there were never no bloodstains when I scrubbed 'em!'

Around is a model village which was built for the workers including an excellent village club which included the first village library supported from the rates. There is still an unexpected treasure. On the wall at the end of the billiards room, the only wall big enough to hang it, is a classical painting showing Atalanta and the Boar Hunt. It is not, as the label claims, by Reubens, but by a group of his students. At least two other versions of the scene are known. It is believed that students painted models from various angles in the studios. The result: a group of paintings which show the same figures but from different viewpoints and in different positions. It ended up here because Ludwig Mond, one of the founding partners, collected outstanding early art. Most of his collection went to the National Gallery where it forms the basis for the Sainsbury Wing. This piece remained in the family until they found they had nowhere big enough to hang it. As a student work and not by the master, it was not considered worthy of the National Gallery and hangs here, almost unknown to art historians.

WINWICK

Its church and village green can hardly be missed, but look out for the pig. On the church tower is a carving of it with a bell hanging from its neck. People say it gave the village its name from its sound of 'oinik' as it moved the stones from the original site to this when they started to build. It more probably kept company with a statue of St Anthony, who lived with a pig in the deserts of Egypt. That was destroyed by the Puritans, but the parish recently put a new St Anthony to keep his pig company.

Inside the church there is part of a huge Saxon cross-head which shows the execution of King (later saint) Oswald by Penda, the pagan King of Mercia, in AD 642. Oswald was shown being executed by being hung upside down. However, when the cross was returned from an exhibition at Liverpool Museum, the men who put it back did not know the tale so put him the right way up – and the cross head upside down! It is possible it happened nearby, for it was said to have been in 'Maserfield' while nearby places like Ashton have the addition of 'in Makerfield'. Penda's son Peada (pronounced Pe-ar-da) was probably responsible for the Sandbach crosses when he became Christian. An unusual possession are the brasses of Sir Piers Legh of Lyme and his wife. They were married as children and he outlived her, then turned to religion. He is depicted wearing armour to indicate his earlier military action but over it he is wearing a priest's chasuble with his coat of arms to show he took holy orders. He holds his hands up in the traditional form for prayer.

 ## WISTASTON

If you visit on most days of the year there is little to distinguish Wistaston from any other village in the district around Crewe but on one day each year it stands out from the rest as the centre of an international competition - the official World Worm Charming Championships. It is held on the grounds around the old primary school and almost any trick can be used to make worms emerge from a given piece of lawn.

It also has one of the quaintest names for an open space: 'Joey The Swan'. Joey lived on a pond in the 1930s and was so tame that he would tap on the windows of the nearby farm when he wanted his breakfast. Although his pond has been filled in, his memory lived on and was used when this area was made into a village recreation area. Wistaston was the childhood home of Elizabeth Minshull in the 17th century. She left for London to be housekeeper for an old blind man. He was John Milton who had been twice married and twice unhappy as a result. He wrote *Paradise Lost* casting Eve as the villain, and *Samson Agonistes* telling of the betrayal by Delilah. Slowly he came to trust women again and married his housekeeper. After his death she returned to the Nantwich district where she gained a reputation for not being extravagant. 'Enough and no more like Mrs Milton's feast', was a proverb in these parts.

 ## WOODHEAD

Woodhead is at the extreme west of the old county in a district called Longdendale, which is noted for a string of reservoirs surrounded by high moorlands. It was an addition to the old county at the end of the 'teapot handle' which was kept as part of Cheshire, separating Derbyshire and Lancashire in the Middle Ages. The salters' road from the Wyches passed this way and it saved paying taxes to another shire when going into Yorkshire, so keeping prices down. There is a small chapel dating from 1487. It has royal and literary associations for the original was built by Edmund Shaa (Shaw) who was a goldsmith to several monarchs and appears in Shakespeare's *Richard III* as the Lord Mayor of London. He also gave Stockport its first grammar school. Above it, on the moors, the railway train to Sheffield enters the second longest tunnel in Britain, which was the longest in the world when it was excavated in 1845.

 ## WOODHEY

Its old hall is long gone, apart from a little arcade which forms a loggia at the end of the private chapel of the Wilbraham family. It is the only church in Cheshire without an altar or communion table for it belonged to a Nonconformist house. Here emphasis was on the sermon so in the middle of the end wall there is a little pulpit, nothing more. The back of it is even more unusual with a screen of rattan hiding an extra row of seats, in which people could stay almost hidden, and it has its own separate access from a stair. It can be viewed by arrangement with the Vicar at Acton. It is in the township of Faddiley, not far from the pretty 17th century 'Thatch' pub - old and attractive but not 15th century as some claim.

This in turn is in the civic parish of Ridley which once had a pool. The Cheshire prophet Robert Nixon must have known Ridley for he said that the pool would become a lane. It was insignificant remarks such as this which were probably written down long after his death that made people of old times take some of his more outrageous predictions seriously. On the other hand he never said when these things would happen so perhaps we are still to see the day when a raven sits on a headless cross in Delamere Forest and drinks the blood of the dead of a great battle. Or when a miller with two thumbs on one hand holds the reins of three kings' horses at the same time.

Drawbridge over the canal at Wrenbury

WRENBURY

In the area are interesting canal drawbridges, like those which Vandyke loved to paint. Its churchyard overlooks a large village green with old cottages. In it the Starkeys and Cottons have their monuments extolling their virtues, including Sir Stapleton Cotton, later Viscount Combermere, who commanded armies in the Peninsular War and in India under the Raj and won battles at Salamanca and Bhurtpore, which became the names of local hostelries. It is his statue on a horse which is outside Chester Castle but his memorial reminds us that 'Paths of Glory lead only to the grave'. Unusually the sanctuary only has one window and contains just a few chairs, giving the gallery of white marble neo-classical allegorical figures representing mourning and salvation the feeling of a mortuary. This is added to by the Victorian bier on which coffins were wheeled to the grave.

By the door is a special pew where the Dog Whipper sat. Many churches employed people to whip dogs out of the church in the 18th century, as they followed owners in when the doors were open and howled along with the hymns or would fight in the middle of sermons. Although his title was 'Dog Whipper' it was one of those which covered a whole host of duties and later became parish beadle. It was one of them who called out to the vicar that he would have to stop part way through the sermon as the bear had arrived for the Wakes. As it was a white one everyone trooped out to see!

My eye was captured by unusual 19th century cast iron epitaphs in the churchyard. They came from the Shropshire iron works along the canal and were made to order. I wonder if they were originally polished with 'black lead'?

WYBUNBURY

Wybunbury Moss is unique, and you must not go near it because it is also dangerous. There is a hidden pool totally covered over by 3 metres of floating peat. It is owned and managed by English Nature because of its importance.

The church is another of those to St Chad said to mark where he preached. The springs here made the little hill unstable and so after several rebuilds a new church was built on a safer site leaving the famous leaning tower as a monument which still attracts visitors. On 26th March 1969 some parishioners were spring cleaning, preparing for a flower festival, when they discovered the Wybunbury silver. No one can tell how long it had been hidden in a chest in the tower. It is kept in a bank vault now and dates from 1790, but is used in the new church for special occasions. The magnificent alabaster monument with effigies of Sir Thomas Smith of Hough and his wife was moved to Nantwich church while the brasses of Ralph Delves and his wife are in the new church. They are mounted on a wall standing in prayer, he in the armour of the time of Henry VII and she wearing a 'kennel head-dress'. The Vicar assured me that in all the time he had been there no one had asked to do a brass rubbing. Then, few people would suspect a new church to hold such an antiquity; an appropriate point on which to end this search for the obscure.